中國體育

SPORT
IN
CHINA

Howard G. KNUTTGEN, PhD
The Pennsylvania State University
MA Qiwei, PhD
Beijing Institute of Physical Education
WU Zhongyuan, BL
China Olympic Publishing House

Editors

Human Kinetics Books
Champaign, Illinois

Library of Congress Cataloging-in-Publication Data

Sport in China / editors, Howard G. Knuttgen, Ma Qiwei, Wu Zhongyuan.
    p.   cm.
  Includes index.
  ISBN 0-87322-193-1
  1. Sports--China. 2. Physical education and training--China-
-History. 3. Sports sciences--China. I. Knuttgen, Howard G.
II. Ma, Qiwei, 1919-   . III. Wu, Zhongyuan, 1926-   .
GV651.S66 1990
796'.0951--dc20
                                            89-49271
                                             CIP

ISBN: 0-87322-193-1

Developmental Editor: Christine Drews
Copyeditor: Dave Dobbs
Assistant Editors: Robert King, Timothy Ryan,
  Julia Anderson, and Valerie Hall
Proofreader: Linda Siegel
Indexer: Sheila Ary
Production Director: Ernie Noa
Typesetter: Sandra Meier
Text Design: Keith Blomberg
Text Layout: Denise Lowry
Cover Design: Hunter Graphics
Illustrations: Craig Ronto and Thomas E. Janowski
Printer: Bookcrafters, Inc.

Printed in the United States of America

10 9 8 7 6 5 4 3 2 1

Human Kinetics Books
A Division of Human Kinetics Publishers, Inc.
Box 5076, Champaign, IL 61825-5076
1-800-747-4HKP

Contents

Preface

It was November of 1980. A patchwork of villages and farms was becoming visible through the scattered clouds below as the plane approached the Beijing airport. My excitement seemed to skyrocket in inverse proportion to our rapid descent. It was difficult to believe that I would soon set foot on the soil of the People's Republic of China, a country enjoying 4,000 years of recorded history but little contact throughout many centuries with the rest of the world.

Images came to mind of the simple agrarian life I had read of 40 years ago in the novels of Pearl Buck. I recalled the countless newsreels during my boyhood of the war and devastation that plagued China from the 1930s through the 1950s. I thought of the Great Leap Forward (1958-1959), the disastrous Cultural Revolution (1966-1976), and the Gang of Four. I knew much about China, yet, because of its vastness in both time and space, I knew so little!

I had been invited along with David Lamb (presently at Ohio State University) by the Chinese Association of Sports Medicine to visit three cities in China on a lecture tour. Much of my excitement stemmed from my curiosity about our Chinese colleagues. Would our reception be relaxed and friendly? Would contact and exchange be easy or difficult? How open would our Chinese hosts be regarding their work, their accomplishments, and the Chinese way of life? Would they share information about both their successes and their shortcomings? Would we establish relationships only as formal colleagues or would we become friends as well?

Our lecture tour was the result of the international relations activities of the American College of Sports Medicine (ACSM). Contact with the Chinese Association of Sports Medicine (CASM) began in 1977 with a routine exchange of scientific journals, and this led to visits by scientists and physicians. Ma Qiwei, coeditor of this book and then president of the Beijing Institute of Physical Education, and contributing author Yang Tianle were the first Chinese representatives to come to the U.S., sent in response to an ACSM invitation to participate in the 1979 annual meeting. Contributing author Weng Qingzhang participated in the ACSM annual meeting the following year. David Lamb and I were the first ACSM representatives to China, sent to present lectures in Beijing, Hangzhou, and Shanghai and to discuss possibilities for expanding our exchange activities.

This visit to China opened a captivating new world for me. I found the history and culture of this great nation fascinating, and the warm reception by our hosts did indeed result in strong and rewarding friendships—and repeated visits! I have now traveled to China on seven occasions, participating in scientific meetings and interacting with many people involved in sports, sports science, and sports medicine.

As Americans and Chinese have come to know more of each other's political systems and cultures, interest in each other's sports, sports medicine, sports science, and physical education has also grown. I felt that the English-speaking peoples of the world interested in these areas deserved an authoritative reference on what was taking place in China. Contact with Ma Qiwei determined that there was great interest on the part of China in introducing the world to China's sport, to tell its history, and describe its present situation. Wu Zhongyuan was invited to join us as third collaborating editor because of his extensive knowledge of sport and unique position as Director of the Press Commission of the China Olympic Committee. We felt that we then had a strong team with which to lead the project forward.

We undertook this project with the objective of presenting a comprehensive overview of all aspects of physical exercise and sport throughout Chinese history, including informal exercise, traditional sports, modern sports, and school physical education. Through many centuries, China was essentially closed to foreign trade and cultural exchange, and little information has been available about its traditions and practices. To gather our information, we enlisted 12 Chinese experts as contributors. Their Chinese manuscripts were translated in China, reviewed by the coeditors, and forwarded to Human Kinetics Publishers for publication as the first comprehensive description of exercise and sport in China.

Part I, Evolution and Organization of Physical Culture, begins with two chapters focusing on the history of sport in China and the development of a new ''physical culture,'' meaning all physical activity undertaken for educational, recreational, health, and competitive objectives. Readers will be fascinated by the games, dances, and military sports of centuries gone by. Chapters 3 through 5 describe the current organization and administration of sport, physical education, and exercise in the community, in the school, and nationwide. The authors detail the hierarchy that organizes programs serving over a billion people. Chapters 6 through 8 cover the traditional and contemporary Chinese sports being played today, with comprehensive coverage of the development of world-class sports and their elite athletes.

Part II, Modern Sports Science and Sports Medicine, is made up of chapters 9 through 13. In this part, contributors review Chinese research in physical education, sports medicine, sports physiology and biochemistry, sports biomechanics, and sport psychology. The history of research is relatively short, but the advancement has been rapid! Descriptions of current activities and projects offer a view of the current state of sophistication and expertise.

In Part III, the Future of Sport in China, the final chapter looks to the future and identifies directions and goals. China's enthusiasm for the development

and advancement of sport would suggest that significant progress and achievement can be expected.

Sport in China should offer a welcome look into the fascinating past and
present of Chinese sport. I hope the book will stimulate further contact and
exchange with the People's Republic of China in the areas of sport and the
sports sciences.

Howard G. KNUTTGEN

Introduction

The history of China is long, eventful, and illustrious. Evidence exists that inhabitants of the area formed villages as long as 6,000 years ago, and the development of a writing system of ideographic characters can be traced back almost 4,000 years. However, China's geographical separation from Western cultures and its intentional isolation from its neighbors have kept secret much information about Chinese civilization and society, even in recent centuries.

As late as 1838, foreign trade was forbidden by Chinese governmental policy, but the military actions of various Western nations opened some cities to international trade in the middle and late 1800s. In spite of this forced exchange, China continued to initiate relatively little contact with the rest of the world.

The Chinese made many cultural achievements during these thousands of years: the development of the writing system, the invention of paper, the construction of architectural masterpieces, and artistic development in painting, music, and dance. Poetry was popular and poets were prolific. Schools of philosophy and religion flourished and survive today by such English names as Taoism and Confucianism. Mathematics and astronomy were highly developed.

Throughout the centuries, the Chinese played recreational games and held contests of physical prowess and military skill. Many of these activities survive in contemporary China, but little has been known by the Western world of their origin and practice.

The early 1900s constituted a period of instability and frequent political chaos for China. A Japanese military invasion and occupation from 1937 to 1945 was followed by 4 years of civil war between the Communist forces of Mao Zedong and the Nationalist forces of Chiang Kaishek. The establishment by Chairman Mao of the People's Republic of China in 1949 introduced a certain political stability that has matured and strengthened despite periods of unrest and hardship. Also during the 1900s, interactions with the outside world introduced China to new sport activities and led it into international competition in such events as table tennis, badminton, volleyball, basketball, soccer, swimming, and track and field.

The tremendous growth in commercial and cultural interaction with China during the past 10 years has made it possible to study how sports and exercise developed there over the course of more than 2,000 years. To place Chinese history in perspective and relate cultural and political events to our own time frame, we present a chronology of important Chinese periods and events (pp. xiv-xv), followed by a timeline of events specific to sport, physical culture, and physical education (pp. xv-xvi). *Physical culture* is the inclusive term used in China for all activities, programs, and benefits associated with physical exercise, games, physical education, and competitive sport. *Physical education* refers more narrowly to public school programs of exercise and sports skills and to the institutes responsible for preparing teachers for this area of the school curriculum.

Throughout the book we have observed the tradition of presenting Chinese personal names with the family name (surname) first and sometimes capitalized.

We invite the reader to learn about sport in China by viewing all its developments in the context of China's unique culture and long history. We present *Sport in China* with the sincere wish for greater understanding, enhanced appreciation, and expanded interaction between the people of China and the rest of the world.

Howard G. KNUTTGEN
MA Qiwei
WU Zhongyuan

Introductory Resources

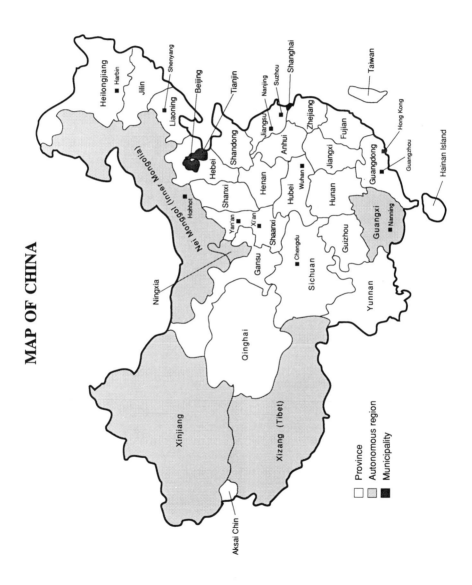

MAP OF CHINA

PERIODS AND IMPORTANT EVENTS
IN CHINA'S HISTORY

Villages formed in northern China	3900 B.C. (approx.)
Xia Dynasty	2100-1600 B.C. (approx.)

Writing system developed, 1900 B.C. (approx.)

Shang Dynasty	1600-1066 B.C.
Zhou Dynasties	1066-221 B.C.
Western Zhou Dynasty	1066-771 B.C.
Eastern Zhou Dynasty	770-256 B.C.
Spring and Autumn period	770-476 B.C.
Warring States period	475-221 B.C.
Qin Dynasty (first unified empire)	221-206 B.C.

Great Wall constructed

Han Dynasty	206 B.C.-A.D. 220

Paper invented, A.D. 105 (approx.)

Six Dynasties (Three Kingdoms period, Western and Eastern Jin Dynasties, Sixteen States period)	220-420
Southern and Northern Dynasties	420-589
Sui Dynasty (China reunified)	581-618
Tang Dynasty (golden age of Chinese Culture)	618-907
Five Dynasties and Ten Kingdoms period	907-960
Song Dynasty	960-1279
Liao Dynasty	1066-1216
Jin Dynasty	1115-1234
Yuan Dynasty (Rule by the Mongols)	1279-1368
Ming Dynasty (China reunified)	1368-1644
Qing Dynasty (Rule by Manchus, descendents of the Tartars; Chinese Empire included Manchuria, Mongolia, Tibet, Taiwan, and the central Asian regions of Turkestan)	1644-1911
Opium War (five Chinese ports forced open by Great Britain to foreign trade; Hong Kong ceded to Great Britain)	1840-1842
Taiping Rebellion against Qing dynasty (much of southern China laid waste)	1851-1864
War with Great Britain and France (dictation by Western nations of the terms of trade relations with China)	1856-1860
Leasing of Chinese cities of Weihai, Quangzhou, and Jiao Xian by Britain, France, and Germany, respectively	1898
Boxer Rebellion (unsuccessful effort to expel foreign influence)	1900
Revolution to overthrow Manchu rule	1911

Republic of China formed (Sun Yatsen first president)	1912
Periods of disunity and provincial rulers	1916-1924
Death of Sun Yatsen and assumption of control by Chiang Kaishek	1925
Split between Nationalists and Communists	1927
Nationalist government (capital in Nanking, later Chungking)	1927-1949
Japanese occupation of Manchuria	1931
Long March of Mao Zedong and Communists	1934-36
War with Japan	1937-1945
People's Republic of China established with capital in Beijing	1949
Nationalists and Chiang Kaishek retreated to Taiwan	1950
"Great Leap Forward"	1958-1959
"Three Years of Hardship"	1960-1962
"Cultural Revolution"	1966-1976
"Period of Reform"	1978-present

IMPORTANT EVENTS IN THE MODERN HISTORY OF CHINESE PHYSICAL CULTURE

First competitive event involving a modern sport in China: track and field meet at St. John's College, Shanghai	1890
German exercises for soldiers adopted by Chinese armies	1895
First basketball game in China held at Young Men's Christian Association, Tianjin	1896
Military exercises introduced to the public schools by the Qing government	1903
Organization of the Far East Sports Association by China, Japan, and the Philippines	1911
First Far East Olympic Games, Manila	1913
China participates in the second Far East Games and earns the most points	1915
Military exercises terminated in the public schools and Western sports and games introduced	1922
Formation of the All-China Physical Education and Sports Promotion Organization	1924
First recognition by the International Olympic Committee of a China Olympic Committee	1931
First Chinese participant in the Olympic Games, sprinter Liu Changchun at Los Angeles	1932
National standards of physical fitness published for the Chinese population according to age groups	1954, 1964, 1974
First Chinese athlete to establish a world record (Chen Jingkai, in weight lifting)	1956

Evolution and Organization of Physical Culture

Part I takes the reader from a period before recorded history to China's entrance into the 1990s. To understand sport in contemporary China, it is necessary to look back at the long heritage of Chinese culture. As described in chapter 1, strong evidence shows that games were common many thousands of years ago. Art objects confirm the practice of organized sport well before the birth of Christ. Interest in early sport activities persists, and the Chinese still practice various forms of these early activities.

Both social and political changes have significantly affected the development of sport. Contact with Western cultures in the 19th century resulted in the introduction of European sports, while internal conflicts, the 1937 Japanese invasion, and the years of civil war that followed suppressed the growth of all sport and organized exercise.

Chapters 2 through 8 trace the development of sport and physical education and describe the present organization of programs for both the public school system and for amateur sport. The authors discuss the objectives of these programs, the training of the teachers and coaches who administer the programs, and the present status of the programs.

Photo on facing page: Many competitive sport activities in ancient China, such as archery and chariot racing, evolved from actual military tasks.

Chapter 1

Introduction to Ancient and Modern Chinese Physical Culture

GU Shiquan

As one of the world's ancient civilizations, China made significant contributions to the world's culture. In physical culture, too, ancient China left a rich legacy. (To Chinese scholars, the term *ancient* refers to the period from remote antiquity to the Opium War of 1840 and the term *modern* to the period from the Opium War to the founding of socialist China on the mainland in 1949.)

Ancient China had no terms corresponding to the *gymnastics* and *athletics* employed in ancient Greece, nor did it have any organized games resembling the original Olympics. However, this is not to say ancient China possessed nothing resembling sport. Terms which originated in early times such as *wuyong* (martial valor), *quanyong* (boxing valor), *xi* (games), *jiji* (art of attacking), and *yangsheng* (the art of keeping fit) give evidence of a thriving physical culture taking numerous forms. The most distinguishing characteristic of these forms is that they were all closely associated with some social activity, such as military training, rituals, sacrifices, medical treatment, or artistic creation.

Ancient Chinese physical culture had its own traditions and was strongly influenced by the country's economy, politics, culture, and philosophical ideas. A rich Oriental flavor was dominant. Modern Chinese physical culture, on the other hand, borrows much from the West.

Primitive Forms of Physical Culture

The earliest signs of Chinese physical culture are found in the caves of Zhoukoudian, where Peking man lived some 500,000 years ago. Here, thousands of skeletons of wild horses and deer suggest the great running ability of these early Chinese. In the Shaanxi province, pellets, bows, and arrows unearthed from the ruins of primitive settlements date back anywhere from 28,000 to 40,000 years. These primitive hunting tools, the earliest specimens of such weapons yet discovered on the mainland, suggest a development of physical culture confirmed at other sites in China by large numbers of ancient primitive weapons, tools, and equipment for games.

These artifacts include mud balls and small marbles that little girls played with and vestiges of dancing, such as the painted figures of dancers on an earthen bowl unearthed in Qinghai province. Dances of ancestors of the Wa nationality, who lived more than 3,400 years ago, are vividly depicted in cave paintings at Cangyuan, Yunnan province. Historical information is also available regarding a kind of dance called *xiaozhongwu* (reduce-swelling dance) used in primitive times to cure leg and foot diseases. From these discoveries and from the study of related documents, fables, and legends, it is apparent that numerous and varied Chinese sports and pastimes of today originate from the skills and lifestyles of people who inhabited the Chinese mainland 3,000 to 4,000 years ago.

Since the establishment of the hereditary system by the Xia Dynasty in the 21st century B.C., over a dozen imperial dynasties have ruled over the lands that make up present-day China. History has seen slave societies, feudal societies, divided kingdoms, and united empires come and go. Thus the magnificent ancient culture of the Chinese nation, including its physical culture, developed and progressed over a tortuous path.

The Influence of Ancient Chinese Physical Culture on Today's Sport Activities

Ancient Chinese physical culture consisted of a large number of different activities and events. These can be classified into three general categories:

- Military sports: archery, chariot races, contests of strength, *wushu* (martial arts), jogging, jumping, throwing, hurling, weight lifting, football (soccer), polo, hunting, tug of war, and swimming
- Medical sports: *qigong* (breathing exercises), *daoying* (fitness exercises, of which there were many forms), massage, *yangsheng* (keeping fit), *fushi* (keeping fit on a diet), *taijiquan* (traditional Chinese shadow boxing), *yijinjing* (exercises to relax the muscles), *baduanjing* (a set of exercises that comprised eight movements, each beneficial to a certain part of the body), manipulation of health-preserving balls, and climbing
- Recreational games and sports: *lishe* (shooting arrows as part of a ceremony or for amusement), *touhu* (throwing darts into a pot), *baixi* (a general term for ancient Chinese songs, dances, and aerobatics), singing and dancing, vehicle racing, horse racing, chess, kite flying, swinging, dragon-boat racing, aquatic sports, ice-skating, hiking, and various other activities during festivals and at temple fairs

Sports That Evolved From Ancient Military Skills

These competitive events constitute the largest subsystem of ancient Chinese physical culture. The roots of these sports extend back thousands of years to the development of certain combat-specific skills. Over time, these skills have evolved into movements and disciplines that serve both as competitive events and fitness exercises for people of all ages.

Development of Martial Arts

The most familiar sport in this subsystem is presently known as *wushu*, but in earlier times was called either *wuyong* (military valor) or *wuyi* (military skill). Present-day wushu may be divided into two categories: the art of fighting bare-handed and the art of fighting with weapons.

As the tactics of warfare evolved, different kinds of military skills appeared to meet different needs. Archery and the use of weapons with long shafts proved practical for fighting from chariots. Archery, fencing, boxing, wrestling, and weight lifting, which developed after the Warring States (475-221 B.C.), were practiced by foot soldiers. Horsemanship, shooting from horseback, and the use of swords and long weapons were activities for

This old silk painting depicts the performance of wushu with a sword.

cavalrymen. By the Yuan and Ming Dynasties (A.D. 1279-1644), these various events had been developed into the so-called "18 kinds of military skills."

If the military skills used on ancient Western battlefields consisted largely of simple blows, thrusts, and parries as means of attack and defense, ancient Chinese military skills were far more complex. They reflected the various elements of classical Chinese philosophy, such as the opposing principles of *yin* and *yang* (negative and positive elements in nature), the "identity of heaven and man" of the Confucian school, and the Taoist concepts of nothingness and silence.

In martial arts, concepts such as *yin-yang*, *kai-he* (open and close), *gang-rou* (strength and suppleness), *dong-jing* (motion and stillness), and *sheng-ke* (to beget and to subdue) were incorporated long ago. Eventually, *neigong*, astrology, and *jingluoxue* (the science of the main and collateral channels of the human body as postulated in traditional Chinese medicine) were also incorporated. (*Neigong* involves breathing exercises to strengthen the internal organs, as expressed in the saying, "Internally, exercise the breathing; externally, exercise the skin, muscles, and the bones.")

All these activities—both battlefield skills and philosophical elements—make up the comprehensive Chinese martial arts system, with its numerous and diverse terms, routines, and movements, its refined skills, and its breathtaking performances.

Firearms became common in battle in the 1300s, and the ancient military skills gradually lost their combat value and evolved into healthful exercises and a kind of performing art. It was then that the name was changed to *wushu*, or martial arts, of which different schools and styles began to appear. Of the many forms and styles of wushu practiced today, about 70 percent originated during the Ming and Qing Dynasties (A.D. 1368-1911).

Today, the martial arts are as popular as ever among descendents of the Yan and Yellow Emperors (legendary emperors regarded as the fathers of the Chinese race) and are spreading rapidly to other parts of the world.

Development of Additional Sports From Military Skills

Jiaoli (wrestling) was variously called *jiaodi*, *xiangpu*, *zhengjiao*, and *shuaijiao* in ancient times. Jiaoli was actually a general term for weight training, especially for the military. Later on, it became an acrobatic exercise. Since the Five Dynasties (A.D. 907-979), it has developed into a sport similar to wrestling.

Running, jumping, throwing, and hurling are track-and-field events today, but in ancient China they were military skills. The modern Chinese character for walking (*zou*) used to mean running. When a nobleman went out riding during the Western Zhou Dynasty, servants or soldiers ran before him. These people were called *xianmazou* (runners in front of a horse) or *maqianzu* (soldiers in front of a horse). During the Spring and Autumn period (772-481 B.C.), there were contests that required soldiers to run 150 kilometers before camping or to run 50 kilometers in full battle dress within half a day.

Jiaoli, ancient Chinese wrestling, is shown in this early wall painting at the Potala Palace in Lhasa, Tibet.

In the Yuan Dynasty, there were races between the imperial guards, called *guiyouchi*, who had to run 90 kilometers (much further than a modern marathon) in six hours.

The high jump and long jump were called *yueju* and *yongyue* in the old days. In the throwing and hurling events, the balls were stones weighing 6 kg each. These skills were required only of the military rank and file. In weight lifting, the weights were the *ding* (a bronze tripod or quadripod that weighed hundreds of kilograms), the bolt of a city gate, a huge rock, or a large iron sword. Lifting these weights also began as a military skill.

Two ball games were popular in China in ancient times: *cuju* or *taju* (a kind of soccer) and *jiju* or *daqiu* (horse polo). Both were forms of military training. A variety of soccer was first played in China during the Spring and Autumn and Warring States periods (770-221 B.C.), earlier than in any other country. In the beginning, it was probably a folk game, but it developed into a kind of military art. In the Han Dynasty (206 B.C.-A.D. 220), the game involved two teams, each of which guarded six goals. During the Tang Dynasty (A.D. 618-907), the number of goals was reduced to two, one for each side, in a game quite similar to modern soccer.

Cuju has been played in China for many centuries, as shown by this Yuan Dynasty (A.D. 1279-1368) painting.

Polo was probably introduced into China from its western regions (historically, an area that extended from west of Yumen Pass to Central Asia). It became a highly developed sport during the Tang Dynasty because of the wars the Tang empire waged against the Turks and other minority nationalities, many of whom were extremely skillful riders. Polo provided military training for cavalrymen as well as entertainment for the nobility. The evolution of *chuiwan* (a variety of golf) was in turn influenced by polo. Chuiwan was played in China long before golf was played in Europe. By the Ming and Qing Dynasties (A.D. 1368-1911), however, the popularity of these ancient forms of football and polo had begun to decline.

A game of chuiwan is depicted in this painting from the Ming Dynasty (A.D. 1368-1644).

Modern tug-of-war originated from the use of a contrivance called *qiangou* used to hook or obstruct enemy ships in ancient naval battles. A grappling hook and line cast onto a nearby enemy ship would be hauled in by a team of men pulling in unison. The enemy ship would be eventually drawn alongside the other ship, and then a boarding party would leap across to engage in close combat. Swimming and fording, too, were originally skills used in battle and belonged to the category of military sports.

Sports That Originated From the Desire for Health and Longevity

These activities were originally designed to cure diseases, promote health, and prolong life. Since very ancient times, the Chinese people have devised various means of enhancing and maintaining physical fitness. The activities include sports or exercises to build up one's physique, cultivate the mind and spirit, and develop the body's latent power. Rich and varied in content, such activities also have a somewhat mysterious quality. It is held that there are secrets of medical science in them that are yet to be understood.

The *qigong* is an example. As early as the Spring and Autumn period (770-476 B.C.), it was said that there were qigong experts who knew how to keep fit by means of breathing exercises. Throughout Chinese history, qigong has been considered an important means of curing diseases, prolonging life, and improving the skills of participants in wushu.

Two other activities that appeared at about the same time as the qigong are the *jingzuo* (sitting in silence or meditation) and *daoying*, which was a

A silk painting from the Xihan Dynasty (206 B.C.-A.D. 24) depicts daoying exercises.

healing art with many forms. Daoying developed from the primitive dance called *xiaozhongwu* and included the *xiongjingniaosheng*, an exercise that consisted of movements imitating a bear climbing a tree and a bird stretching its wings. It was developed during the Spring and Autumn and Warring States periods (770-221 B.C.). Such exercises are depicted in the silk painting of daoying exercises unearthed from a Han tomb at Mawangdui. Also depicted are the *wuqinxi* (an exercise imitating the movements of tigers, deer, bears, apes, and birds) of the Three Kingdoms period, the ''24 Sitting Postures'' of the Song Dynasty (A.D. 960-1279), and the *taijiquan* and *baduanjing* of the Ming (A.D. 1368-1644) and Qing Dynasties (A.D. 1644-1911).

Taijiquan exercises are still popular in China today with people of all ages, such as these retired workers exercising at dawn in a city park.

In addition, the hygienic practices that began during the time of Confucius, consisting of the massage of the Sui (A.D. 581-618) and Tang as well as the *fushi* (practice of good nutrition) of the Southern and Northern Dynasties (A.D. 420-589), fall into the category of activities for health and longevity.

Games and Sports That Developed for Recreation and Entertainment

Games of this category were popular among both the nobility and the common people in ancient China. Many of them have had long histories. These include the games of *weiqi* (Go) and *xiangqi* (Chinese chess), which are now well known throughout the world. Also included are flying kites, rowing dragon boats, ice skating, playing on a swing, and racing horse-drawn carriages. People participated in these activities in China over 2,000 years ago.

Weiqi has been a popular recreational activity in China for many centuries, as this painting from the Tang Dynasty (A.D. 618-907) shows.

Demonstrations of athletic skills at banquets, during sacrifices, or in honor of a guest are also sports of this category. Two such sports deserving mention because of their distinct Chinese characteristics are the *lishe* and *touhu*.

Lishe, the ceremonial shooting of arrows, began in the Western Zhou Dynasty (approximately 1000 B.C). It was a ritual activity engaged in largely by the aristocracy. Different occasions required the use of different kinds of bows, arrows, and targets, as well as different music and attendants. A strict division of social ranks and classes existed, with rules and regulations that had to be carried out to the letter. The etiquette of the event was considered far more important than the competition. This unique form of archery or ceremonial shooting was more a demonstration of feudal ethics than a sport.

Touhu ("throwing into a pot") which evolved from archery, was a game of throwing darts into a pot or kettle placed at a distance. It was a contest usually played at banquets by feudal nobles. The size of the target kettles varied greatly and many different techniques of throwing were employed.

With the passing of time, these two variations of archery gradually lost their significance and disappeared from the stage of history.

These drawings illustrate various targets used in lishe.

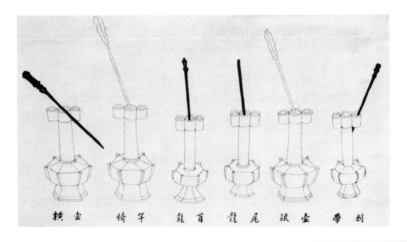

Many different forms of pots and darts were used in touhu.

The Introduction of Foreign Sports Into Modern China

The gates of China were closed to the outside world until the Opium War of 1840, when the British opened them with opium and guns. During this stage, sports in China, like China itself, underwent great changes. Western sports were introduced into China from Europe, America, and Japan, while many of China's traditional sports, such as wushu, wrestling, archery, and qigong, continued to develop.

Preserving and Developing Traditional Sports

In the modern era (1840-1949), traditional Chinese sports were perpetuated through two main channels; one was through folk sports and the other through the army and the public schools.

The Role of the Common People

Wushu, wrestling, qigong, and other traditional sports were deeply rooted in the Chinese populace by the 19th century. The semifeudal Chinese society, with its self-sufficient economy, made it difficult for Western influence to penetrate into the vast mountainous areas and rural areas. In addition, many workers, clerks, and townspeople of the lower classes accepted the influence of Western sports very reluctantly. These factors encouraged the preservation of traditional Chinese sports.

Folk sports such as the traditional martial arts (wushu) were indispensable in nearly all the people's armed struggles. These included the Guangzhou Uprising against the British in 1841; the Taiping Heavenly Kingdom (1851-1864); the Nian Army, or the Torch Bearers, a peasant army that rose against the Qing government in the middle of the 19th century; and the Yihetuan Movement, an anti-imperialist armed struggle waged by North China peasants and handicraftsmen in 1900. Even after the 1911 Revolution, traditional sports played a major part in some secret societies and underground groups. Chinese traditional sports also remained important as features of traditional holidays (such as the Spring Festival), temple fairs, and other celebrations.

The Role of the Military and the Public Schools

During the Opium War, the army of the Qing Dynasty (1644-1911) was equipped with fowling pieces, indigenous guns, and other firearms as well as swords, cudgels, spears, and other hand weapons. Because the Qing soldiers also resorted to Chinese boxing or wrestling in close combat, wushu and other traditional sports continued to constitute a major part of military sports.

This state of affairs began to change in the 1860s. As foreign guns and cannons were introduced into China, wushu and other traditional military sports were gradually replaced by Western military drills. However, wushu and other traditional sports weren't totally withdrawn from the army. As late as the 1930s, army units still looked on wushu with favor. Wushu enjoyed great popularity among the Northwest Army under the command of Christian General Feng Yuxiang. General Ji Hongchang, for instance, one of Feng's generals, was famous for promoting wushu in his garrisons in Ningxia and Gansu provinces. The Japanese Army became panic-stricken when confronted with the fighting team armed with broadswords under the command of General Song Zheyuan during the Resistance Campaign at the Great Wall in the 1930s. Wushu, wrestling, and other martial arts have since been preserved in the armies led by the Guomintang and the Communist Party of China. Chinese boxing, wrestling, grappling, and other combative techniques have remained obligatory courses for all soldiers engaged in guard duty, security, reconnaissance, arrest, surprise attack, and other special tasks. The preservation of these skills has continued despite a growing Western influence on China's military and athletic practices.

With the abolishment of the imperial system of education and the introduction of Western educational systems at the beginning of the 20th century, Western military drills and gymnastics were adopted as the major form of physical education in the public schools of China. After 1915, organized track-and-field, ball games, swimming, and other events appeared in school children's extracurricular activities, and the Western style of sports competitions began to develop at schools.

However, wushu, wrestling, and other traditional sports were preserved as part of the physical education courses at schools, where the "National Military Education Program" was implemented for approximately 25 years. Around 1918, a kind of "New Wushu," an exercise made up of separate movements adapted from wushu, was developed by an army officer named Ma Liang. The Northern Warlords' Government (1912-1927) considered it an obligatory exercise in Chinese style for all people at colleges and schools and in the learned circles to practice all over the country. This directive was carried out all over China. Until the 1940s, wushu and other traditional sports remained integral components of most physical education courses.

A Move Toward Western Military Exercise and Physical Education

Military exercises were the first Western sports activities introduced into China. During the 1860s, the bureaucrats of the Qing Dynasty, who initiated the Westernization Movement, started buying foreign guns and cannons from Europe and America. They also invited foreign instructors to drill the new armies in Western military exercise. Among them were the Xiang Army (Hunan province) headed by Zeng Guofan, the Huai Army (Anhui province) headed by Li Hongzhang, and the New Army headed by Zhang Zhidong.

The 1898 Constitutional Reformists, with Kang Youwei, Liang Qichao, Yan Fu, and others as their representatives, introduced the Western bourgeous educational ideal of all-round development (moral, intellectual, and physical), an ideal they found embodied in German military exercises and Western physical education programs. They put these programs into practice in new schools such as the "Straw-Shed-among-Wood School" in Guangzhou and the "Current-Affairs School" in Hunan province.

The beginning of the 20th century brought the end of the imperial examination system and the establishment of what were called "new-type schools." In these schools, two or three hours a day of military exercise were required of every student. Many a low-ranking military officer was invited to coach at the schools.

These courses were dropped from public school curricula in 1922. Since then, track-and-field, gymnastics, ball games, and other Western sports have been established as the main content of physical education classes at primary schools and high schools. This signalled a major change from the imitation of Japanese and German school systems to the imitation of American schools.

Physical education classes in elementary schools incorporate many skills from Western games.

The physical exercise course was renamed "physical education course," and the term physical exercise coach replaced by "physical education teacher."

The Effects of Christianity and Travel Abroad on Modern Sports

Modern Olympic events and sports competitions were introduced into China through the following channels:

- The Christian church system, which set up a number of Christian missionary schools as well as the Young Men's Christian Association (YMCA) and the Young Women's Christian Association (YWCA)
- Chinese studying or working abroad (e.g., baseball was introduced from the U.S.A. into China by the famous railway engineer Zhan Tianyou)
- Foreigners (mainly diplomats) visiting China

Christianity was introduced into China in 1807. By 1916, as many as 7,088 church centers, cathedrals, and churches were established. As a result, quite a number of Christian missionary schools as well as YMCA's and YWCA's soon spread all over China. These institutions were not only enthusiastic promoters of modern sports, but also administrators of many early competitions.

Generally speaking, there were no formal physical education courses at the Christian missionary schools, but there were many extracurricular sport activities and competitions inside and outside the school. The year 1890 witnessed the first intramural track-and-field games held in China, at Shanghai's St. John's College. Beginning in 1899, sports meets were held annually between St. John's College and the Nanyang Public School. Later on, games were also held in schools in Tianjin, Nanjing, Suzhou, Beijing, and other cities. Finally, the First All-China Colleges and Schools Sports League Games (subsequently recognized as the First National Games of China) were held in 1910. The North China Games were held 18 times during the period from 1913 to 1934. The YMCA and YWCA played a major role in the organization of many of these events.

The Western influence in athletics eventually went so far that China's athletic world became dominated by foreigners. Sports organizers, coaches, and referees at athletic competitions were all foreigners; regional and national sports organizations were established and managed by foreigners; and foreign priests handled the preparations and arrangements for the Far East Games. Even the heads of the physical education departments at Chinese colleges and the leaders of Chinese sports teams sent abroad were foreigners. It was an American who made a speech on behalf of China at the opening ceremony of the Sixth Far East Games in 1923.

Development of Physical Education and Sports During the 1920s and 1930s

The period from 1927 to 1937 brought huge strides in Chinese sports. The influence of visiting foreigners and of Chinese who had studied abroad brought an increasingly systematic approach to physical education. National programs such as the Ministry of Education's Physical Education Committee and the Physical Education Inspector Program took responsibility for standardizing physical education in colleges and schools. A National Conference of Physical Education was convened. Other signs of the increasing emphasis on physical education were the Law of Physical Education, the Plan for Implementation of the Physical Education Program, and a set of decrees and regulations concerning public physical education programs. These programs established the first nationwide standards for physical education and resulted in substantial progress in the training of teachers, the acquisition of teaching materials, and the organization of competitions and other extracurricular sports activities.

To encourage international competition, the All-China Physical Education and Sports Promotion Association was established in 1924, and China became a member of the International Olympic Committee in 1931. This created a growing emphasis on organized competition. The fourth, fifth, and sixth National Games, together with as many as 18 North China Games and 6 Central China Games, were held during this time. Provincial and municipal games also made progress, and large stadiums were built all over China. A number of outstanding athletes appeared and many new records were established. This development came to a premature end in 1937 when the War with Japan commenced.

The ensuing period saw a decline in physical education and sports in China. After 8 years of the War With Japan and 3 years of civil war, China's physical education and sports programs were in a chaotic state. So bad was the situation that the athletes from North China who had participated in the seventh National Games were unable to return home. The Chinese athletes taking part in the 14th Olympic Games in London couldn't pay for their return traveling expenses.

Physical Education and Sports in the Revolutionary Bases During the Revolutionary War and the War With Japan

When cooperation between the Guomindang (the group that eventually established itself on Taiwan) and the Chinese Communist Party broke down in 1927, the Chinese Communist Party carried on with its strategy of encircling the cities from the rural areas. It methodically established many small revolutionary bases in remote mountainous regions. These bases were separated and often surrounded and attacked by both the Guomindang Army and, later, the Japanese Army and its puppet troops during the War with Japan. Even so, the Workers' and Peasants' Democratic Government strived to promote physical education and sports so that they could better fight and win the Revolutionary War.

The largest of the revolutionary bases in China during the 1931-1934 period was in the Southern Jiangxi and Western Fujian provinces, with Ruijin as its center. As the National Congress of Workers, Peasants, and Soldiers was held and the Central Workers' and Peasants' Democratic Government was formed, physical education and sports became highly developed here.

First of all, sports closely connected with military skills were organized in the ranks of the Red Army. These included running, mountain climbing, swimming, high jump, long jump, obstacle racing, basketball, and volleyball. Also played at the company clubs of the army (called "Lenin Rooms" at the time) were table tennis and chess and other board games. Military sports were popular among young people outside the army, too. These sports included cudgel play, spear play, and broadsword play. Basketball and volleyball were played mainly by party and governmental officials.

The Red Army men and the local people in this region often held athletic games or sports competitions on such occasions as Women's Day (March 8), Labor Day (May 1), Youth Day (May 4), and Army Day (August 1). The First Chinese Soviet Republic Games were held on May 30, 1933. Immediately after that, the Red Physical Culture Association, a special organization in charge of physical education and sports in the region, was set up.

Mao Zedong, Zhu De, Deng Xiaoping, Nie Rongzhen, and other leaders led the participation in sports. Even along the 12,500-kilometer Long March (1934-1936), when Mao led his supporters to Shaanxi province to organize the liberation movement, there were occasional sports activities among the Red Army men.

After the Red Army arrived in North Shaanxi province at the end of the Long March, the Central Committee of the Chinese Communist Party settled at Yan'an and stayed there for 13 years. The Shaanxi-Gansu-Ningxia Border Region was set up as the national revolutionary nerve center from 1935 until 1948. During that period, physical education and sports were even more highly developed in Yan'an and the Shaanxi-Gansu-Ningxia Border Region than they had been during the Ruijin period. The Yan'an Physical Culture Association and the Yan'an New Physical Education Society were established, and the Physical Education Department of Yan'an University was instituted to train physical education and sports cadres. The large-scale Yan'an September 1 Sports Meet was held in 1942. As young intellectuals from the Guomindang-controlled region poured into Yan'an following the outbreak of the War with Japan in 1937, many cadre schools and sports personnel sprang up in Yan'an.

The Yenan Tower in Shaanxi overlooks this public sports complex where many organized sporting events and recreational activities are held.

As a result, sports and athletic activities grew even more frequent and larger. They were also conducted in a more scientific and standardized manner, and skill levels were higher than during the Ruijin period.

During the War with Japan, the Red Army, redesignated as the Eighth Route Army and the New Fourth Army, remained the center of sports activities in the Red region. Of the Eighth Route Army units, the 120th Division under the command of He Long was the one where sports activities were most highly developed. Its "Fighting Basketball Team" emerged as the unbeatable champion all through the base area.

Athletic activities were also taking place in the headquarters of the Eighth Route Army under the command of General Zhu De, even in the days of fighting against the Japanese. A sports meet was held in 1941 by the 129th Division under the command of Liu Bocheng and Deng Xiaoping. The New Fourth Army, while fighting successively in different areas north and south of the Yangtse River, also had sports activities.

Major Events in the History of Physical Culture

China's long history contains many events that either promoted the development of physical culture or altered its orientation. The following are some of the more important ones from the author's point of view. Note that because in ancient times sports could hardly be separated from other social activities, it is sometimes difficult to determine the exact time and place a certain historic event began or ended.

Events in Ancient Times

China's first schools were set up during the Xia Dynasty (21st-16th centuries B.C). The school system was completed during the Western Zhou Dynasty (11th-7th centuries B.C.). Courses equivalent to modern physical education were gradually formed, among them archery, chariot-driving, and dancing.

Guan Zhong, assigned Prime Minister of the State of Qi in 685 B.C., vigorously promoted the development of boxing. It is said that Chinese boxing was originated in the State of Qi, in Shandong Peninsula.

After unifying the six warring states in China in 221 B.C., the first emperor of the Qin Dynasty ordered that all weapons in the former states be handed over to the central government. He also prohibited the people from practicing martial arts of any kind. This had a devastating effect on the development of military sports.

In 140 B.C., Emperor Wudi of the Han Dynasty ruled that only Confucian philosophy and a few selected classics were allowed to be studied at schools. Because a gentle and quiet character and a delicate physique were Confucian ideals, a physical education was basically excluded from school curricula.

In 702 A.D., Empress Wu Zetian of the Tang Dynasty initiated an imperial cadet examination, establishing a precedent of selecting elite performers according to their skill in the martial arts. This inspired a standard of physical fitness and skills among military officers and contributed to the popularization of martial arts among the people.

Starting with the Song Dynasty (A.D. 960-1279), when firearms became popular for military use, the role of the "cold weapons" (those without gunpowder) diminished. The martial arts began to be seen less as a military skill and more as an art and a healthful discipline. This gradually brought forth the concept of wushu.

After the Song Dynasty, Lixue, a Confucian school of idealist philosophy popular in the Song and Ming Dynasties and advocated by scholars Cheng and Zhu, prevailed as an official school of philosophy. Lixue recommended "stillness" and advocated the "Three Cardinal Guides" (ruler guides subject, father guides son, and husband guides wife) and the "Five Constant Virtues" (benevolence, righteousness, propriety, wisdom, and fidelity). Lixue respected literary talent but belittled military prowess. This discouraged the development of physical culture to the extent that China was once labelled the Sick Man of the Far East.

Since the Ming Dynasty (A.D. 1368-1644), various wushu techniques with different weapons and apparatus were gradually standardized. An all-round champion was considered one skilled in the use of eighteen kinds of weapons. Wushu became more and more complicated and attained higher levels of development and standardization.

These farmers are performing wushu with shovels, which substitute for weapons.

Rulers of the Yuan Dynasty (A.D. 1279-1368) and the Qing Dynasty (A.D. 1644-1911) prohibited the practice of martial arts and discouraged the development of folk sports. As a result, some of the traditional Han people's sports, such as cuju (a kind of football), jiju (horse polo), and touhu (a game of throwing darts into a pot or shooting arrows into a picher) have been lost. Meanwhile, sports popular among the ruling classes were further developed. Among these were riding, archery, wrestling, skating, and a soccerlike game played on ice.

Events in Modern Times

When Tsarist Russia presented Western guns and cannons as gifts to the Qing Government in the early 1860s and sent Russian instructors to train the

Qing imperial guards, Western military exercise for soldiers was formally introduced into China.

In 1890, a sports meet with track-and-field as the principal events was held at Shanghai's St. John's College. It was the earliest sports meet ever held in China.

Starting in 1895, the New Armies of China began to drill soldiers in German military exercise. German exercises with a strong component of gymnastics became popular for soldiers.

In 1896, the first Chinese basketball match was held at the Tianjin Young Men's Christian Association.

In 1903, the Qing Government promulgated "The School Regulations Approved by His Majesty the Emperor," which promoted military exercise in the public schools.

In 1915, China participated in the Second Far East Games and won the highest total score of all the nations. This spurred the development of modern sports and sports competitions in China. Public schools started extracurricular sports activities, and physical education in schools began advancing on a double-track system, with military exercises emphasized inside class and modern sports outside class.

In 1922, military exercise was totally withdrawn from Chinese schools when the Northern Warlords' Government of China promulgated a new educational system, the "Renshu Educational System," together with the "Course Standards of the New Educational System," which was an imitation of the United States' educational system as opposed to the systems of Germany and Japan. Track-and-field, gymnastics, children's games, and other sports became the main content of the standard school physical education curriculum. This was an event of great importance.

In August 1924, the All-China Physical Educational and Sports Promotion Association was organized to promote the development of modern sports and sports competition. The Association became a member of the International Olympic Committee in 1931.

On May 30, 1933, the First Chinese Soviet Republic Games, the first large-scale athletic meet for the Communist revolutionary bases, was held in Ruijin, Jiangxi province. Right after that, the Red Physical Culture Association, the first of its kind in the Red region, was set up.

Beginning July 7, 1937, when the War with Japan broke out, sports in the Guomindang-controlled areas began to decline. By contrast, physical culture and sports in the Shaanxi-Gansu-Ningxia Border Region, the largest revolutionary base with Yan'an as its center, were thriving and climaxed in 1942 when the Yan'an September 1st Games were held.

Summary

Taking a sweeping look back at 4,000 years of physical culture in China, we see a complicated picture full of twists and turns. Many sports that are rich in content and so bright in form remain from China's ancient traditions. Full of striking national features, these traditional sports contain a valuable heritage that deserves to be both preserved and further developed. This heritage is supplemented by other sports learned from abroad. These sports have taken root and now play a leading part in China's physical culture. Together, traditional sports and Western sports form a sort of yin and yang, at once antithetical and complementary to each other.

It should be pointed out that throughout China's history, both ancient and modern, the broad masses of laboring people were often not the masters of their own lands. At times the thriving and declining of physical culture or the rise or fall of a sport depended upon the likes or dislikes of those in power. At such times, China's physical culture had to develop within the confines of this class minority, and the broad masses of workers and peasants were either denied access to physical education and sports or restricted from participating fully in these activities. The exception was in the revolutionary bases, where the laboring people became masters of the land under the leadership of the Chinese Communist Party, as well as of their own physical education and culture.

This state of affairs spread from the revolutionary bases to all of China in 1949, when the socialist New China was founded on the Chinese mainland. A new epoch in the history of physical culture development in China thus dawned on the Oriental horizon.

Photo on facing page: The Beijing Workers' Stadium has a seating capacity of 80,000.

Chapter 2

Physical Culture in the New China

XIE Qionghuan

After the founding of the People's Republic of China in 1949, physical culture became an important component of the socialist state. The constitution of the People's Republic of China stipulates that the state should develop physical culture and promote mass sports activities to build up the people's physique and that the state should promote the all-round moral, intellectual, and physical development of children and young people. To accomplish these aims, the government's yearly budget includes funds for promoting physical culture. In 1985, the state allocated 600 million yuan (approximately 300 million U.S. dollars) for the promotion of exercise and sports. This does not include funds for the construction of large stadiums and gymnasiums.

The Increasing Number of Sport Organizations, Facilities, and Equipment

After more than 30 years of construction, a national sports headquarters and service center has come into being in southern Beijing. Located in contiguous buildings are the State Physical Education and Sports Commission, the All-China Sports Federation, the China Olympic Committee, the Chinese Society of Sports Science, the National Research Institute of Sports Science, the General Office of *Sports News*, the People's Sports Publishing House, the Sports Photo Publishing House, and the editorial offices of several sports magazines, such as *New Sports* and *China Sports*. The complex also includes the China Sports Service Company, the Sports Hotel, the Beijing Gymnasium, and the Longtanhu Stadium.

In old China, there were very few stadiums and gymnasiums. Today, the number of stadiums, gymnasiums, swimming pools, and floodlit courts with fixed bleachers, as well as sports grounds suitable for mass sports activities, exceeds 410,000. The number of stadiums has increased 20 times; gymnasiums 18 times; swimming pools 21 times; training halls 34 times; and sports grounds 55 times the numbers existing in 1949.

The Beijing Workers' Indoor Stadium seats 15,000 people.

Sports equipment has also multiplied both in number and in type, while quality has improved and sales have risen dramatically. For instance, the table-tennis balls of Shanghai's "Red Double Happiness" brand and Guangzhou's "Double Fish" brand, the footballs and basketballs of Tianjin's "Golden Cup" and Shanghai's "Train" brands, the volleyballs of "Train" brand, and the barbells of Shanghai's "Lishi" brand have all been chosen for formal international competitions by world sports organizations. Designs and production of sportswear, sports shoes, and sports equipment have been steadily improved and those products are being exported to other countries. Only 30 years ago, the country had to import every item of competitive sports equipment, including the whistles employed by game officials.

The establishment of organizing bodies for the various sports, the construction of stadiums and gymnasiums, and the production of sports equipment and sportswear have provided the necessary material conditions for the development of China's sports.

The Influence of Government Personalities and Organizations

Many prestigious revolutionaries of the older generation, including Mao Zedong, Liu Shaoqi, Zhou Enlai, Zhu De, and Deng Xiaoping, showed great concern for sports development. They often participated in various sports activities, such as swimming, table tennis, taijiquan, weiqi, go chess, running, and

Mao Zedong, Zhou Enlai, and Deng Xiaoping (shown, from right to left, attending the 1955 National Workers' Games), and other founders of the People's Republic of China paid great attention to the development of sport in China.

calesthenic exercises. They received and encouraged athletes, coaches, and other sports workers who had made great contributions to the country's sports cause.

Various Communist Party and government leaders have been made honorary presidents of national sports associations. At present, Ulanfu, vice-president of the People's Republic of China, is the honorary president of the China Equestrian Association. Vice-premier Wan Li is the honorary president of the China Tennis Association. Xi Zhongxun, member of the Secretariat of the Communist Party of China (CPC) Central Committee, is the honorary president of the China Badminton Association. Yang Shangkun, vice-chairman of the Military Commission of the CPC Central Committee, is the honorary president of the China Table Tennis Association, and Peng Chong, vice-chairman of the National People's Congress Standing Committee, is the honorary president of the China Gymnastics Association.

Usually, the State Physical Education and Sports Commission calls a meeting at the beginning of each year that is attended by the heads of the sports commissions of the country's provinces, municipalities, and autonomous regions, as well as the presidents of sports institutes attached to the State Physical Education and Sports Commission and the Commission's department directors. The purposes of the meeting are the review of the experiences of the past year and the planning of the objectives and activities for the coming year. Representatives from the State Education Commission, the All-China Federation of Trade Unions, the Central Committee of the Chinese Communist Youth League, the General Political Department of the Chinese People's Liberation Army, the All-China Women's Federation, and sports associations of various industries are invited to the meeting to enlist their close cooperation for the development of China's sports.

The social status of sports workers has gradually improved with the development of the sports themselves. Many workers have taken an active part in discussions of the Communist Party, state affairs, and policy. Li Menghua, minister in charge of the State Physical Education and Sports Commission, is a member of the CPC Central Committee; Deputy Minister Yuang Weimin is an alternate member of the CPC Central Committee; and the famous athletes Li Furong, Li Ning, Chen Zhaodi, Han Jian, Han Aiping, Chen Zude, Li Cuiling, and Zhao Changjun are deputies in the National People's Congress. The famous athletes Zhang Rongfang, Nie Weiping, Zheng Minzi, and Li Shulan, as well as the well-known coaches Huang Jian, Huang Qianghui, and Yang Rensui, are members of the Chinese People's Political Consultative Conference. These and other representatives from the sports world air their opinions, raise problems related to sports development, and propose suggestions and demands at the meetings of the CPC Central Committee, the National People's Congress, and the Chinese People's Political Consultative Conference. Many prominent sports personalities have been assigned to leading positions in mass organizations, including the Chinese Communist Youth

League Central Committee, the All-China Women's Federation, and the All-China Youth Federation.

Objectives for Sport in Chinese Society

As sport organizations and sports workers grow in number and power, establishing like goals becomes more important. Four general objectives for sport in China are

- developing and maintaining good health,
- developing new leaders for Chinese society,
- promoting the development of the socialist economy, and
- enhancing relationships with other countries.

An analysis of each of these goals follows.

Developing and Maintaining Good Health

A primary function of sports in China is to maintain the people's fitness. As early as 1952, Chairman Mao assigned this task to the sports workers, saying: "Promote physical culture and build up people's health." Chinese sports personnel and organizations ever since have striven to improve the physical conditions of the Chinese population and erase the image of China as the Sick Man of the Far East.

China is a developing socialist country. The government has done its best through the years to make it easy for the people to take part in sports and to encourage them to improve their health. The Education Program promulgated by the State Education Commission stipulates that physical training is required of all school pupils up to the second year of university study. Students are required to have two physical education classes each week. In addition, the students take part in extracurricular physical training and sports activities in accordance with their own interests. Sports activities and exercise groups in both urban and rural areas have grown in both size and number. Medically therapeutic sports, elderly sports, handicapped sports, and sports tours have sprung up one after another. According to recent statistics, 300 million people in China take part in various sports activities. More than 120 million Chinese have attained or surpassed standards of physical training set up by the state.

Since the late 1940s, the average life expectancy for a Chinese person has doubled, from 35 to 70. During the period 1979 through 1981, large-scale surveys of the size and fitness of Chinese children and youth were conducted by the State Physical Education and Sports Commission (also referred to as the State Physical Culture and Sports Commission), the State Education Commission, and the Ministry of Public Health. Comparing those findings with similar data from 1955, the study found that the average height of boys between the ages of 7 and 18 had risen at a rate of 2.3 centimeters for every 10 years and that of girls 2.1 centimeters for a like period. In addition, boys' average weight increased by 1.35 kilograms and the girls' weight by 0.92 kilograms. In sports performance, all age groups markedly improved their scores in the 50-meter dash, the 1500-meter run, the standing long jump, and in chin-ups.

These results show a remarkable improvement in the physique of Chinese children and youth in the past 30 years. Much of the improvement is due to improving economic conditions and nutrition. However, it is also due to extensive participation in sports activities.

Developing New Leaders for Chinese Society

Physical culture has always been regarded as an important means of education in Communist China. Young people are expected to develop physically as well as morally, intellectually, and aesthetically.

When he was young, Mao Zedong published a famous thesis, "Study of Physical Culture and Sports," which appeared in the April 1917 issue of the journal *New Youth*. In the thesis, Mao Zedong pointed out that

> physical training shares the importance with moral education and intellectual development. But moral education and intellectual development are based on physical training. Without physical development, there will be no basis for moral and intellectual education. . . . Sports embody morality and are a means to carry intellectual knowledge. Sports are like a wagon to carry knowledge and a shelter for morality.

Chinese sports administrators are well aware of the importance of physical culture in education. The standard teaching program stipulates in explicit terms that physical education should develop in its students a love of the socialist motherland, a sense of morality and of individual and collective discipline, and a spirit of determination and dauntlessness.

Physical education teachers have developed great expertise in realizing these goals. Endurance sports are used to foster students' strength of spirit. Competition and team play cultivate a sense of collective honor and the virtues of unity and mutual effort. This can also help the students adopt healthy attitudes about the relationship between the individual and the collective, and toward failure and victory. High-skill sports such as gymnastics and skating are used to instill respect for aesthetics and discipline. To cultivate civilized behavior and manners, students are asked to prepare and collect equipment before and after class. This also teaches students the value of physical labor and to take good care of public property. Through such methods, physical training becomes not only a means of keeping fit but also a form of moral education. It strengthens students' characters and fosters their sense of social responsibility.

Promoting the Development of the Socialist Economy

Chinese sports authorities realize that the quality of the labor force depends on both the intellectual and physical strength of the workers. Physical training obviously improves the workers' health, which is assumed to increase resistance to disease and thereby reduce medical expenses. Physical training also improves the intellectual level of the workers. It helps the workers master production skills faster and increases attendance and productivity.

Examples of Economic Improvement

The Liming Machinery Plant in Shenyang, in Liaoning province, employs 20,000 workers. In the first half of 1976, the workers took a total of 133,203 days for sick leave, reducing production and causing estimated economic losses of 6.39 million yuan (approximately 3 million U.S. dollars). When sports activities were subsequently initiated at the plant, the workers' health improved remarkably. Total sick-leave days in the first half of 1979 were down to 77,771, roughly half the 1976 level, and 1982 saw a further reduction. Meanwhile, productivity rose markedly.

Emergence of New Industries

The growth in sports in China has given birth to a number of new industries. These new industries and trades—primarily the manufacture of sports facilities and apparatus, the development of related services, and jobs in sports science and technology—have developed steadily as the improvement of the standards of living throughout China makes it possible for people to spend more money on sports. Thus, sports-related trades and products play an increasingly important role in the state economy. As the Chinese economy becomes more privatized, quite a few stadiums and gymnasiums have converted from state operations to private or semi-private business enterprises. The development of sports recreation, sports travel, and sports convalescence has not only augmented state revenue but has also promoted development of the country's light industry, food processing, transportation, communications, and tourist industries.

Enhancing Relationships With Other Countries

With China following the policy of opening itself to the outside world, sports are playing an ever greater role in strengthening the unity and friendship between the Chinese people and the people of the other countries. Motivated by the Olympic spirit and a desire to promote world peace and progress, Chinese sports organizations actively conduct exchanges and cooperative activities with other countries. This strengthens the unity and friendship between Chinese and foreign athletes and peoples. China presently conducts sports exchanges—activities involving athletes, coaches, and sport teams from China, interacting with those from more than 150 countries and regions in Asia, Europe, Africa, Oceania, and the Americas. In the first half of the 1980s alone, more than 3,000 sports exchange events involving over 30,000 people took place. Because sports exchanges often herald formal diplomatic ties between China and other countries, Chinese athletes are often praised as a ''diplomatic vanguard.''

A slam dunk by a player on the Chinese men's basketball team, which has won many Asian championships.

China hosts several international competitions every year. In 1983 alone, China hosted international track-and-field, soccer, and swimming tournaments, as well as the First Asian Cup Table Tennis Tournament. The Chinese capital, Beijing, is now building more facilities for the 11th Asian Games in 1990. At the same time, China is creating the necessary conditions for hosting the Olympic Games and World Cup Soccer Tournament at future dates.

China makes energetic efforts to take part in international sports affairs. Presently, China has membership in 65 world sports organizations and 33 Asian sports organizations. Seventy-three Chinese sports authorities have assumed leading positions in 53 international organizations. For instance, He Zhenliang, vice-minister in charge of the State Physical Education and Sports Commission, is an executive member of the International Olympic Committee, vice-president of the Olympic Committees Association, and vice-president of the Presidium of the International Congress of World Sports Federations. The famous table tennis player Xu Yinsheng, also a vice-minister in charge of the State Physical Education and Sports Commission, is vice-president of the International Table Tennis Federation. In these organizations, Chinese representatives work together with their colleagues from other countries to promote mutual understanding and create new prospects for international sports.

Since the 1960s, China has helped dozens of countries to build 42 stadiums, gymnasiums, and other sports facilities. These include the Mogadishu Stadium in Somalia, Siaka Stevens Stadium in Sierra Leone, the Independence Stadium in Gambia, and other sports facilities in such countries as Syria, Pakistan, Burma, Libya, and Morocco. Referring to the Moroccan project, the Moroccan prime minister said, "The comprehensive sports facilities are an outstanding achievement. It is the fruitful result of the Moroccan-Chinese friendship and the orientation of North-South cooperation. It's our pride, as well as yours." President Juan Antonio Samaranch of the International Olympic Committee said: "Whoever goes to Africa can see the first-rate stadiums and gymnasiums constructed by China." In recognition of such contributions, the International Olympic Committee awarded China the Olympic Cup.

China has dispatched thousands of coaches and sports workers to nearly 100 countries to help them develop sports and raise the level of competition. The coaches are specialized in more than 20 events in which Chinese athletes excel, including table tennis, badminton, gymnastics, volleyball, basketball, track-and-field, weight lifting, handball, and diving. Many world champions and world record breakers, such as Xi Enting (table tennis), Liang Geliang (table tennis), and Ni Zhiqin (high jump), have coached in other countries where they were warmly welcomed by the local athletes and people.

In 1987, the Chinese soccer team traveled to Brazil for training. Chinese soccer player Xie Yusin was invited to join a Division II Soccer Club in The Netherlands. Chinese sports medicine experts, scientific researchers, and physical education teachers have also increased contacts with their counterparts in other countries. By attending meetings and giving lectures abroad, they have strengthened mutual understanding, learned much from others, and contributed to the improvement of international sports competition.

The development of sports in China and the contributions of China to world sports have earned high praise from other countries. The International Olympic Committee awarded Chinese vice-premier Wan Li the Olympic gold medal for service to sport and silver medals to vice-presidents Rong Gaotang and

Vice-Premier Wan Li received a gold medal from the International Olympic Committee in 1986 as presented here by IOC president Samaranch.

Huang Zhong of the All-China Sports Federation as well as Zhong Shitong, former president of the China Olympic Committee.

Fundamental Steps in the Development of Physical Culture and Sports

In the early years of the People's Republic, China laid emphasis on the development of mass sports activities with the aim of improving the health of all people. When this proved successful, high-level sports training was added to the agenda, with an emphasis on the Olympic events.

Funds, Organization, and Guidelines for Sport

In capital construction, allocation of funds, and development of scientific research, priorities were given to those organizations that trained athletes for participation in the Olympic Games. This emphasis continues today. To raise the level of such events as track-and-field and swimming, the state has appropriated special funds for the construction of facilities with synthetic track surfaces and indoor swimming pools in many parts of the country. It has also encouraged local authorities to improve training in these events.

Meanwhile, the effort to extend sports training to all segments of the population continues. Sports organizations have been established in education, health, agriculture, and forestry departments, as well as in trade unions, the Communist Youth League, women's federations, and other mass organizations. In addition, the state has encouraged industrial enterprises, social organizations, institutions of higher learning, and individuals to undertake and support sports.

Guidelines have been gradually instituted to coordinate various developmental activities. In the early 1950s, *Sports System in Preparation for Labor and Defense of the Country* was published to establish ranking systems for athletes and coaches and provide regulations for grass roots sports associations. Exercises to radio music and work-break exercises have helped to popularize sports in the early years of the People's Republic.

After the 1960s, *The Sports System in Preparation for Labor and Defense of the Country* was revised and titled *The National Standards of Physical Training* (see Table 4.1). These standards outlined the country's goals for the enhancement of young people's health and encouraged them to take part in regular exercise in an effort to enhance their physical development and improve their sports capability.

Chinese authorities subsequently developed and published the *Skill Ranking System for Athletes*, *Skill Ranking System for Referees*, *Regulations for Athletes*, *Regulations for Coaches*, *Regulations for Referees*, *Provisional Regulations of Technical Titles for Coaches*, and many other rules and regulations guiding competitions. These encourage athletes and sports workers to strive for outstanding achievements and win honor for the motherland. At the same time, the institution of standardized rules and regulations has stabilized the management system and so improved the management of competitive sports.

Rewards for Sport Participation

Both moral encouragement and material reward are granted to those athletes, coaches, and scientific researchers who make remarkable achievements. The awards are given not only to the medal winners at the Olympic Games, Asian Games, National Games, and other major international competitions, but also to the coaches and administrative departments who have trained these champion athletes. The State Physical Education and Sports Commission confers the Honorable Medal of Sports on those who make outstanding contributions to the country's sports development. Between 1981 and 1985, a total of 429 people won this honor. To provide an impetus for track-and-field and swimming, the Commission recently established annual gold and silver medals to reward excellence in these events.

In 1979, the Chinese press recognized the 10 best athletes in the country. This then became an annual activity. The 1984 contest involved more than 1.6 million people. In 1985, certain provinces began to recognize their own 10 outstanding athletes. In addition, the mass media in Beijing lists the 10 major sports news items of each year. Such activities have encouraged

Chinese athletes to scale new heights in world competition, improved the social status of sports in China, and strengthened relations between those in the sports world and other walks of life.

Interest in sports has also been increased by the designation of various "homes of sports" (centers of popularity for and sources of great contenders in particular sports), as well as model sports families. Today in China there are several hundred homes of sports, including the home of volleyball, home of track-and-field, home of martial arts, home of swimming, and home of football (soccer). There are also several hundred counties that have been designated as advanced counties of sports, such as Putian County in Fujian province, the "Home of Track-and-Field," Taishan County in Guangdong province, the "Home of Volleyball," and Dongguan County of Guangdong province, the "Home of Swimming." To encourage schools at all levels to make greater contributions to the country's physical culture, outstanding physical education teachers are selected and schools with outstanding sports programs are recognized. These schools are offered enhanced opportunities for competition.

Sports and the Media

The active nationwide dissemination of sports knowledge has helped more people gain a deeper understanding of sports and sports development and led to greater involvement in sports activities. *Renmin Bao* (or *People's Daily*, the leading newspaper in China), has a regular sports column and its yearly coverage amounts to one million Chinese characters. The English-language paper *China Daily* devotes a full page to sports in China and other countries every day. The China Central Television network regularly broadcasts sports programs. *Sports News*, the country's leading sports paper, has a circulation of 600,000. The magazine *New Sports* has a circulation of 930,000. The English magazine *China Sports* is on sale in 107 countries and regions around the world. The People's Sports Publishing House released 152,000,000 copies of sports books between 1981 and 1985. At present, China publishes a total of more than 100 sports newspapers and magazines.

Strengthening Research

To strengthen sports science research, the Chinese Research Society for Sports Development Strategy was set up in 1985. The talents of Chinese sports experts and scholars is pooled to study the key problem in Chinese sports science and technology. These personnel also offer consultation to administrative departments for decision making. Other sports-science research institutions have been established to conduct research on basic and applied sports-science

China's numerous sports magazines have played an important role in the dissemination of sports knowledge.

theory to ensure the continued improvement of training methods. Modern scientific instruments have been used to raise the quality of training programs.

All these efforts have paid off, ensuring a steady development of sports in China. The country has become one of the leading nations in the international sports community of Asia, and the gap between China and the sports powers of the established world is being narrowed.

Challenges and Goals in China's Sports Future

The development of sports in China during the past 30 years provides evidence of both successes and shortcomings. Valuable lessons have been learned that provide guidelines for the future. China has been forced to deal with three sport-related issues:

- The detrimental effect of governmental overconcentration on individual initiatives.
- The conflict between traditional and modern sports.
- The problems of training for high-level sport in a developing country.

Governmental Overconcentration Versus Individual Initiative

During a fairly long period after the founding of the People's Republic, a system of highly unified and concentrated administration of sports was practiced in China. The State guided sports development with policies, decrees, and plans. Funds for sports activities were allocated by centralized government departments. In an economically underdeveloped country, this practice is advantageous in that the application of manpower, material, and financial resources can be concentrated through government adjustment and control. It ensured China's early sports development.

However, with the change to a planned commodity economy in the 1980s, Chinese sports administrators have come to realize that such overconcentration yields contradictions that are difficult to overcome. One of the major problems is that overconcentration and centralization can discourage less centralized institutions from pursuing or developing an interest in sports management. A monolithic managerial pattern results in inflexible competition systems. Presently, one of the objectives in the ongoing reform of the sports system is to find a balance that can maintain the advantages of socialist centralization while providing other parts of society with the initiative to engage in sports.

Industrial enterprises, social organizations, and institutions of higher learning should be encouraged to manage their own sports programs and competitions. Collectives and individuals are now allowed to conduct commercialized sports enterprises. Efforts are being made to promote diversification of sports. Sports not only constitute a social project but also a business. Different approaches can be taken to encourage such new projects, including providing financial assistance, establishing sports foundations, and combining sports with business activities.

Traditional Versus Modern Sports

While making efforts to develop modern sports, China also pays attention to the development of its traditional sports. China is a multinational country with a population of over one billion people. Besides the Han (94% of Chinese population), there are more than 50 minority nationalities, each of them having certain favorite traditional sports. In such a large nation, the levels of both economic development and quality of sports competition vary from place to place. Therefore, it is impossible and unnecessary for all parts of the country to develop the same modern sports. China has attempted to combine modern sports with the traditional ones while respecting regional differences.

Traditional sports are extremely popular in the vast rural areas and the regions inhabited by distinct ethnic groups. Quite a few traditional sports events have developed further after being systematized, reformed, and improved. For instance, wushu (martial arts) has long been valued by the government and society and has absorbed the interest of people around the world.

Minority nationalities' sports meets have been held in Tianjin, the Inner Mongolia Autonomous Region, and the Xinjiang Uygur Autonomous Region. On holidays and festivals, traditional sports demonstrations are held in many places around the country. By developing modern sports and maintaining traditional sports, China remains one of the world's most diverse and colorful sports communities, and this should ensure that it will make still greater contributions.

Training for High-Level Sport

To expedite the training of outstanding athletes, leisure-time training networks connecting all levels of competition have been organized throughout the country. Sports teams are organized into three echelons similar to the A, B, and C leagues of American amateur-league play. All sports teams are required to train athletes with high goals in mind and to enhance their advancement to the highest levels of competition. In training, a three-level system has been adopted consisting of grass-roots sports teams, leisure-time sports schools, and outstanding sports teams. Organizational measures establish and maintain relations among the three so that, while they have separate tasks, they also have close relations. The child athlete receives systematic, scientific training from the beginner's level all the way through to participation on a high-level team.

The system has proved highly effective in encouraging talent. Among the 24 Chinese gold medalists at the 23rd Olympic Games, 21 had gone through the three-level training system. Nearly all of the athletes representing China in the 24th Olympic Games were products of this system.

In the early 1950s, China adopted the Soviet Union's Sports System for its labor and defense forces. After several revisions, it evolved into the State Physical Training Standards. These standards have played an active role in promoting sports development among young people.

In competitive sports, advanced techniques and strategies from other nations have been introduced selectively around the country. At the same time, creativity and innovation are encouraged. For instance, the Chinese women's volleyball team once trained according to the system created by Hirofumi Daimatsu, coach of the former world champion Japanese team, and also employed techniques and strategies from other championship teams. The "time difference" (interval between setting and spiking) has been adapted to enrich the quick-spiking techniques developed by China's players. The women's team also has tried the men's skills, such as "flat," changing positions, and "drifting." Using these techniques, the Chinese women's volleyball team has become one of the best in the world, equally proficient at offensive and defensive play. The Chinese table tennis team has also retained its own unique skills while learning from the strengths of other teams. The Chinese gymnastics team has also profited from the experience of foreign counterparts, developing skills with difficult, new, and elegant movements.

Summary

China stresses that sports should help build socialist material and cultural civilization. Athletes, coaches, and referees as well as other sports workers are always educated to be socialist new people with lofty ideals, high moral standards, cultural knowledge, and discipline. They are imbued with a spirit of patriotism, internationalism, and sportsmanship, with a particular emphasis on unity and friendship.

Physical culture and success in sports are important factors in the international identification of a nation. Compared with many sports powers, China, beginning from a low starting point, still has a long way to go. While striving to display her talents and learning from other countries, China must constantly explore new ways to develop sports in accordance with her own conditions.

Photo on facing page: The Tiyuguan Road complex in Beijing houses many of the agencies that govern or serve physical culture and sports in China.

Chapter 3

Organizational Structure of China's Physical Culture

WU Zhongyuan and QUE Yongwu

In this chapter, the long evolution of the administrative organization of China's sport network will be studied. The genesis of the fascinating relationships that exist among traditional Chinese sports, martial arts, and modern sports will be explored and explained.

Sport Organizations in Ancient and Modern China

Individual sport organizations began to develop as participation in particular activities became popular and widespread. For the purposes of standardizing techniques and governing actual competition, sets of guidelines and regulations were developed and groups were recognized as governing bodies for particular sports.

Associations in Ancient China

Sports organizations in martial arts and other traditional sports existed long before modern sports were introduced. These organizations were loosely formed associations. Most of them were independent and factional.

Organizations in Modern China

Modern sports—such as the Olympic and other international sports common to various countries of the world—were introduced to China at the turn of the 20th century. With them came the emergence of regional and national sports organizations.

Local Organizations

The first such organizations were linked with revolutionary activities against the rule of the Qing Dynasty. One example is the Sports Association of Shaoxing, Zhejiang province, which was founded by Xu Xilin and his wife, Qiu Jin, both well-known revolutionaries between 1905 and 1907. This association assembled students from schools in Shaoxing once a month to perform physical exercises with the objective of spreading democratic ideas among them and inspiring their morale to revive the nation. Apart from promoting sports, the organization served as a cover for both overt and clandestine revolutionary activities.

This kind of organization also emerged in the large cities such as Shanghai, Guangzhou, and Beijing. The movement then spread to medium-sized cities and overseas communities in which Chinese lived. Among them, the Jing Wu Sports Association was the most famous and enduring. It was founded in Shanghai in 1910 by China's famous martial arts master, Huo Yuanjia. Later, branches were organized in Shaoxing, Hankou, and Guangzhou, as well as in southeast Asia.

Dr. Sun Yatsen, the great pioneer of Chinese democratic revolution, wrote a monograph entitled *Spirit of Martial Qualities* in 1919 for the Jing Wu Sports Association to mark its 10th anniversary. The Association taught wushu as its main activity advocating a scientific approach to the national art and instruction in it for millions of people, thus promoting the development of China's martial arts with great impact both at home and abroad. Later, the Jing Wu

Sports Association encouraged the development of modern sports such as ball games and swimming.

The All-China Sports Promotion Association

China's first national sports organization, the All-China Sports Promotion Association, was founded in Nanjing in 1924 by personnel drawn mainly from educational and foreign affairs circles. At that time, sport courses were offered widely in the country's primary and middle schools, national sports meets were held, and Chinese athletes were sent to participate in the Far East Sports Meet to compete with athletes from Japan and the Philippines. It became both necessary and possible to establish a national sports organization, and the All-China Association filled that need.

Wang Zhengting, a well-known diplomat, and Zhang Boling, an educator, were elected president and vice-president of the Association. Wang Zhengting would later become the first Chinese member of the International Olympic Committee.

The tasks of the All-China Sports Promotion Association were to conduct exchanges on sports issues with other nations through correspondence, to draw up rules for various amateur sports, to organize regional soccer matches, and to host the Far East Sports Meet in China. The Association also published sports periodicals, helped make arrangements for national sports meets, and selected athletes to participate in both the Far East Sports Meet and the Olympic Games. However, the organization could not play a more important role for various reasons. Chief among these were the wars in China during the 1930s and the 1940s. In 1949, some of the members of the Association moved to Taiwan. The Association was subsequently reorganized into the All-China Sports Federation.

Sport Organizations in the People's Republic

After the founding of the People's Republic of China, an authoritative national sports system was established. This system includes four major organizations:

- The All-China Sports Federation is the nationwide mass sports organization.
- The State Physical Education and Sports Commission is a governmental organization directly under the leadership of the State Council.
- The China Olympic Committee is the leading body for the promotion of Olympic events in China.
- The China Sports Science Society is the leading organization in the field of sports science.

The All-China Sports Federation
and Its Grass Roots Sports Associations

Great political and social changes took place at the end of the 1940s as the People's Republic of China was founded following the victory of the people's revolutionary struggle. During this period, many of the leading members of the All-China Sports Promotion Association left the mainland to live in Taiwan or elsewhere abroad. As a result, the organization's activity was completely suspended. In October 1949, the leading members of the Association who had stayed in mainland China met in Beijing with various other personnel active in sports. With a strong desire to establish an effective national leading agency, they decided to reorganize the All-China Sports Promotion Association into the All-China Sports Federation. They elected Professor Ma Xulun, a famous educator and social activitist, as the first president of the Federation and Rong Gaotang as the first secretary-general.

The All-China Sports Federation became the sole national sports organization responsible for the development of China's physical culture. The Charter of the All-China Sports Federation adopted in 1952 at the second Congress of the Federation stipulates that the specific functions of the Federation were to

- develop programs for China's physical culture;
- formulate and publish rules and regulations concerning specific sports activities;
- take charge of liaison work on physical culture and sports with other nations;
- hold national sports meets and select and train athletes of various events for national teams;
- collect and examine books and periodicals on sports;
- publicize physical culture information among the broad masses of China's people;
- train administrative leaders for programs of physical culture; and
- design and examine major sports facilities and sports equipment.

The All-China Sports Federation has branches in various provinces, autonomous regions, municipalities, autonomous districts, counties, and autonomous counties. The Federation has also set up sports associations at the grass roots level by establishing units at factories and mines, business enterprises, institutions, schools, villages, and neighborhoods. The Federation includes as institutional members national associations of various sports events, the Sports Committee of the Chinese People's Liberation Army, and the sports associations of various industries and trades. The Federation has played a major role in promoting the development of China's physical culture. Among its presidents were Dr. Ma Yuehan, a well known physical educator, and Zhong Shitong, former president of Beijing Physical Culture Institute.

The Capital Indoor Stadium in Beijing has a seating capacity of 18,000.

From 1949 to 1958, the All-China Sports Federation also served as the China Olympic Committee.

With the founding of the State Physical Education and Sports Commission (see pp. 47-50), the All-China Sports Federation changed its functions. The Fourth Congress of the All-China Sports Federation, held in February 1964, decided that its tasks should be to

- organize the country's amateur sports activities;
- unite the sports workers and athletes of the country;
- advocate and promote mass sports activities throughout the country;
- hold national sports competitions; and
- host or participate in international sports events.

The All-China Sports Federation has evolved into a national sports organization that is of nongovernmental, social, and mass character. The current president is Li Menghua, who is also minister in charge of the State Physical Education and Sports Commission.

Under the leadership of the All-China Sports Federation, sports associations were set up in different industries and trades in order to attract and organize people to take part in sports activities. For instance, the China Locomotive Sports Association was founded by railway workers and staff; the China Coal Mine Sports Association by coal miners; and the China Qianwei Sports Association by personnel of the public security system. These sports associations have set up central offices as well as local and grass roots organizations, some of which have full-time staff. Besides organizing workers, staff, and family members to participate in their own sports activities, these associations also organize teams to take part in sports meets held by their trade organizations and to engage in regional and national competitions.

Sports associations of various industries and trades were very active in the mid-1950s. A total of 19 sports associations from various national industries and 25,100 sports associations of more local basis were established, with a total of 1.68 million members by the end of 1956. The China Locomotive Sports Association, for example, established a complete set of organizations at different levels, from the administrative railway bureaus and subbureaus down to the basic units of stations, sections, and factories. This association boasted more than 200 full-time and over 1,400 part-time administrators.

At the first Workers Sports Meet, held in Beijing in October 1955, more than 1,700 athletes from over 20 industries participated in track-and-field, cycling, weight lifting, basketball, volleyball, soccer, and other events. During the 10-year period of the Cultural Revolution (1966-1976), most of these sports associations suspended their activities, which set back the workers sports movement considerably.

In the 1980s, sports associations in the industries and trades began to resume their activities. At present, sports associations have been reorganized

As vice president of the All-China Sports Committee, He Zhenliang (left) has played an important role in the development of sport in China. Another vice president of the All-China Sports Committee, Xu Yinshen (right) has also been instrumental in China's rapid sport advancement.

in eight industries: railways, coal mines, petroleum, forestry, banks, water conservation and electric power, construction, and public security. Preparations are being made to organize sports associations for other trades.

Sports associations are a primary instrument in the development of mass sports activities. The associations have trained many excellent athletes. For example, the women's field hockey team of the China Locomotive Sports Association was China's champion team in 1987.

The All-China Sports Federation is also a member of the International Congress of Sports Federations. He Zhenliang, an executive member of the International Olympic Committee and vice-president of the All-China Sports Federation, is presently vice-president of the Presidium of the International Congress.

The State Physical Education and Sports Commission

The State Physical Education and Sports Commission is a ministry of the Chinese government in charge of physical culture and operates directly under the leadership of the State Council. It is headed by a minister who holds a cabinet level position. The Commission was founded on November 15, 1952, by a decision of the Central People's Government Committee. Its first minister was Marshal He Long, a well-known revolutionary and strategist who was concurrently vice-premier of the State Council and vice-chairman of the Central Military Commission. Following the founding of the State Physical Education and Sports Commission, local sports commissions were organized in provinces, municipalities, autonomous regions, and counties.

The minister in charge of the State Physical Education and Sports Commission is nominated by the State Council and appointed by the Standing Committee of the National People's Congress. Besides Marshal He Long, Wang Meng also held the position. Wang Meng had been engaged in army political work for a long time and held the posts of political commissar of an army and of a greater military area. From 1953 to 1980, Rong Gaotang and Huang Zhong were vice-ministers in charge of the State Physical Education and Sports Commission. They have been awarded silver medals by the International Olympic Committee for their contributions to the development of China's physical culture. The long-term minister in charge of the State Physical Education and Sports Commission was Li Menghua, who is also president of both the All-China Sports Federation and the China Olympic Committee. Vice-minister He Zhengliang is an executive member of the International Olympic Committee. The other two vice-ministers are Yuan Weimin and Xu Yinsheng. The latter was formerly a well-known table tennis player and coach. The only female vice-minister at this time is Zhang Caizhen, who has worked in the area of physical culture for more than 30 years.

Zhang Caizhen (left) is the only female vice minister of the State Physical Education and Sports Commission. Yuan Weimin (right) is another vice minister of the State Physical Education and Sports Commission.

Tasks of the State Physical Education and Sports Commission

The "Organic Rules of the State Physical Education and Sports Commission," as approved by the Standing Committee of the State Council of the People's Republic of China in March 1956, stipulate that under the leadership of the State Council, the State Physical Education and Sports Commission is responsible for leading and supervising the country's sports activities. The national government assigned the Commission to

- administrate the enterprises, institutions, mass organizations, and schools directly under the Commission and direct the work of local sports commissions;
- guide, coordinate, and supervise the physical cultural work of various departments, trade unions, and other social organizations;
- carry out the State Physical Exercise Standards, develop mass sports activities, and improve the skills of athletes;
- develop a national plan for sports competition, hold national sports meets, supervise the organizational work of sports competitions held by various departments and social organizations, and approve national records in various sports events;
- maintain contacts with international sports organizations, host international events, and organize athletes to participate in international competitions;
- formulate and approve rules for sports competitions; examine and approve teaching programs, textbooks, and teaching materials for physical culture; and, together with the educational department, examine and approve teaching programs, textbooks, and teaching materials for physical education in the schools;

- establish sports science research institutes and arrange sports science research;
- cooperate with departments concerned with the preparation of teachers and specialists in physical culture and supervise various departments and social organizations in training and assigning sports administrators;
- organize medical supervision for physical culture in cooperation with the Ministry of Public Health;
- disseminate sports information;
- develop plans for building stadiums and gymnasiums as well as rules for their use;
- assist in the development of plans for the production of sports equipment, including the supervision of their use and approval of appropriate specifications and standards; and
- formulate grading rules for athletes, coaches, and referees; formulate rules for conferring honorary titles on athletes, coaches, referees, and other sports workers; and award state honorary medals of sports.

Obviously, the national and local physical culture and sports commissions are the authoritative leading bodies of sports in China. However, the State Physical Education and Sports Commission is not responsible for physical education in the schools, which is the responsibility of the State Education Commission, nor does it regulate military sports, which are overseen by the Ministry of National Defense.

Departments and Institutions in the State Physical Education and Sports Commission

The State Physical Education and Sports Commission is comprised of the following departments:

Administration Department: Oversees routine organization and coordination of other departments.

Mass Sports Department: Develops mass sports.

Competition and Training Department No. 1: Governs shooting, motor, sports, aeronautical sports, aquatic sports, archery, and cycling.

Competition and Training Department No. 2: Governs all ball games.

Competition and Training Department No. 3: Governs track-and-field events, swimming, skiing and skating events, and mountaineering.

Competition and Training Department No. 4: Governs gymnastics, weight lifting, fencing, wushu, and chess.

International Liaison Department: Oversees relationships with other nations and international organizations and the organization of international sports activities.

Sports Science and Physical Education Department: Oversees sports research institutes and sports institutes.

Information and Publicity Department: Generates and oversees sports publicity.

Finance and Planning Department: Plans major sports undertakings and the construction and production of sports facilities and equipment, as well as their financing.

Personnel Department: Assigns and assesses administrative personnel for physical culture programs.

Policy Study Office: Reviews and suggests necessary changes in sports policies.

Institutions directly under the State Physical Education and Sports Commission consist of:

Training Bureau: Organizes and trains national sports teams.

Sports News Publishing House: Publishes the newspaper *Sports News.*

New Sports Publishing House: Publishes the magazine *New Sports* and other sports periodicals.

China Sports Publishing House: Publishes the English monthly magazine *China Sports.*

Office in Charge of Foreign Aid: Assists in the construction of sports facilities in other countries.

Research Institute of Sports Science: Conducts and coordinates scientific research on sports and exercise.

China Sports Service Company: Arranges commercial sports activities such as travel and accommodations for sports teams.

In addition, the China Martial Arts Research Institute and the China Chess Institute are presently being established.

Six out of the country's thirteen sports institutes of higher learning are directly responsible to the State Physical Education and Sports Commission. Those are the Beijing Institute of Physical Education, the Shanghai Institute of Physical Education, the Wuhan Institute of Physical Education, the Xi'an Institute of Physical Education, the Chengdu Institute of Physical Education, and the Shenyang Institute of Physical Education.

The China Olympic Committee

The China Olympic Committee is a national organization with the aim of developing sport in China and promoting the Olympic Games. The Committee publicizes and promotes the Olympic movement and its goals in China. It represents China in relations with the International Olympic Committee and the Olympic committees of other countries.

The China Olympic Committee was recognized by the International Olympic Committee in 1931. However, China had contacts with the International Olympic Committee (IOC) much earlier than that. When the IOC was founded in 1894, Baron Pierre de Coubertin, its founder and first secretary-general, wrote the Qing government to invite China to take part in the first Olympiad held in Athens, Greece. China failed to participate because the Qing government, among other things, did not take the matter very seriously.

By 1920, the IOC had formally recognized the Far East Sports Association organized by China, Japan, and the Philippines. Wang Zhengting, a Chinese diplomat and an organizer of the Far East Sports Association, was elected the Chinese member of the International Olympic Committee in 1922.

During the 1930s and 1940s, the China Olympic Committee sent athletes to the 10th Olympiad held in Los Angeles in 1932, the 11th Olympiad in Berlin in 1936, and the 14th Olympiad in London in 1948.

Before the 1932 Olympiad was held, the Chinese Guomintang government at first declared that China would not enter the 10th Olympiad. The Japanese Army had invaded and occupied China's three northeast provinces and plotted to send athletes designated by Japan to take part in the Olympiad on behalf of the so-called Manchu state. When this news was leaked, public opinion both at home and abroad was rigorously opposed to the plot. With the financial aid of general Zhang Xueliang, Liu Changchun, a famous sprinter from northeast China who had fled the Japanese occupation to Shanhaiguan, went to Los Angeles and participated in the Olympiad on behalf of China. This was the first athlete China sent to the Olympic Games.

Chinese athletes did not win any medals in the Olympiads held in 1932, 1936, and 1948, as the quality of sports competitions in China during this period was quite low. At the time, China was nicknamed the Sick Man of the Far East. This designation was related to China's backward physical culture and sports and her accompanying failure in international sports competitions.

After the formation of the People's Republic of China in 1949, the China Olympic Committee told the IOC that China would like to send a sports delegation to the 15th Olympiad to be held in Helsinki, Finland, in 1952. After many difficult negotiations, the Organizing Committee of the 15th Olympiad finally sent an invitation to China. The Chinese sports delegation, headed by Rong Gaotang and with Huang Zhong and Wu Xueqian (now the Chinese foreign minister) as deputy heads, took part in the Olympiad. This reestablished normal relations between the China Olympic Committee and the IOC.

Unfortunately, when Avery Brundage of the United States became president of the International Olympic Committee in 1954, he admitted the Olympic Committee of the Republic of China (i.e., the Chinese Nationalist government of Taiwan) into the International Olympic Committee. Thus the serious issue of "two Chinas" was created. The representative of the China Olympic Committee repeatedly urged the Committee to recognize (in conformity with the Olympic Charter) only one national organization of China—the China Olympic Committee. However, the proposal was rejected by the International Olympic Committee, and in protest the China Olympic Committee suspended its contact with the International Olympic Committee in 1958. The suspension of this relationship was most unfortunate for both sport in China and for international sports competition.

After over 20 years of controversy and negotiation, the IOC finally recognized the legitimate seat of the China Olympic Committee in November 1979 with 62 votes for, 17 against, and 2 abstentions. The resulting resolution stipulates that the name of the Olympic Committee of the People's Republic of China is the "China Olympic Committee" and that the national flag and anthem of the People's Republic of China will be used in all ceremonies. This meant that the name of the Olympic Committee in Taibei (Taiwan) would be the "Chinese Taibei Olympic Committee" and the flag, anthem, and emblem formerly used by them could not be so used in the future. A new flag, anthem, and emblem for Chinese Taibei have since been approved by the International Olympic Committee.

Since the resolution of this issue, China's international sports exchanges and activities have developed rapidly. In 1982, China sent a delegation of more than 400 people to take part in the Ninth Asian Games in New Delhi, India. Chinese athletes won 61 gold medals. For the first time in the history of the Asian Games, China captured more gold medals than did Japan, which once dominated the Asian sports. At the 10th Asian Games in 1986, China again won more gold medals than any other nation.

In 1984, a Chinese sports delegation participated in the 23rd Olympiad in Los Angeles, and Chinese athletes won 15 gold, 8 silver, and 9 bronze medals. This was the first time in China's sports history that Chinese athletes won gold medals at an Olympiad. It was widely considered a major breakthrough. At the 1988 Olympics in Seoul, China again showed its strength as Chinese athletes won 5 gold, 11 silver, and 12 bronze medals, for a total of 28 medals.

The China Olympic Committee is playing an increasingly more important role in the International Olympic Committee. He Zhengliang, the Chinese member of the International Olympic Committee, was elected an executive member of the IOC in 1986. Also in 1986, the International Olympic Committee awarded an Olympic gold medal to Wan Li, vice-premier of the Chinese government, who had actively promoted Olympic sports in China. It also awarded Olympic silver medals in 1983, 1984, and 1986, respectively, to Rong Gaotang, Zhong Shitong, and Huang Zhong, all well known figures in Chinese sports.

The delegation of the People's Republic of China parades in the opening ceremony of the 23rd Olympiad in Los Angeles.

Li Menghua, a top Chinese official, is president of the China Olympic Committee.

Under the leadership of current president Li Menghua, the China Olympic Committee is actively contributing its share to the International Olympic movement. In 1990, China will host the 11th Asian Games in Beijing. The China Olympic Committee plans to bid for an Olympiad at the beginning of the next century.

The China Sports Science Society

China organized its first national sports science conference in 1978. People engaging in sports science and technology proposed at this time the organization of an academic organization for Chinese sports science personnel. The aim was to unite and organize all scientific and technical personnel of various trades throughout the country who were engaged in or enthusiastic about research in the science of sport, physical cultural education, training, sports management, and the production of sporting goods, to conduct academic exchanges both at home and abroad and to popularize sports science and technology. The organization would also offer the government opinions on major decisions and policies concerning sports science. The proposal drew attention from many quarters in China.

The 1980 National Symposium on Sports Science was held in Beijing on December 15, 1980, and became the founding meeting of the China Sports Science Society. About 500 scholars and authorities attended the meeting, which was an unprecedented gathering in the history of China's sports science and technology.

During the past 6 years, the China Sports Science Society has developed rapidly and established 12 subsocieties, including those of sports scientific theory, sports training, sports medicine, sport psychology, sports biomechanics, sports information, physique research, sports equipment and apparatus research, sports statistics, sports construction, physical education research, and the application of computer techniques. The Society has also established 26 branches at the provincial level and accepted nearly 8,000 members, mostly lecturers, engineers, attending physicians, and coaches.

The China Sports Science Society carries out its work under the guidance and support of the State Physical Education and Sports Commission. The highest governing body of the China Sports Science Society is the National Congress, which is held every 5 years. The executive organ is the Council. During its 5-year term, a Standing Council composed of the president, the secretary-general, and other members handles the council's affairs. The president of the China Sports Science Society is Huang Zhong, a veteran sports worker, vice-president of the All-China Sports Federation, and winner of an International Olympic Committee silver medal.

Current vice-presidents of the Society are Zhang Caizhen (vice-minister of the State Physical Education and Sports Commission), Zhao Bin (former vice-president of Beijing Institute of Physical Education), Du Haoran (director of the Department of Science and Education under the State Physical Education and Sports Commission), Ma Qiwei (professor of Beijing Institute of Physical Education), Lu Shaozhong (director of the National Research Institute of Sports Science under the State Physical Education and Sports Commission), and Qu Mianyu (president of Beijing Medical University). The secretary-general is Que Yongwu.

Academic Contributions

The Society has developed along with China's general physical culture. It, in turn, has provided great help to the advancement of the country's sports activities. Over the past 6 years, the Society has organized and carried out more than 360 academic events attended by more than 33,000 scientific workers. Over 5,000 scientific and clinical papers have been presented at these meetings, covering a wide range of subjects involving sports theory, physical education, sports history, physical testing, sports statistics, sports training, sports biomechanics, sports physiology and biochemistry, sports traumatology, medical monitoring, medical sports, sport psychology, and sports equipment and apparatus. The papers demonstrated a high academic level whether on the design of experimental plans, the application of experimental techniques, data processing, or deductive reasoning.

Of these papers, 30 have been presented awards by the State Physical Education and Sports Commission. The first prize ever given was in 1982 to the paper, ''A General Description of the Physical Shapes, Functions, and Qualities of Chinese Children and Youth.'' Data were presented on 23 indexes as tested on 183,414 students from 1,210 universities, middle schools, and primary schools in 16 provinces and cities. A total of 4,410,936 items of data were obtained. For the first time, fairly comprehensive basic scientific data on the physique of China's youth were collected, data that were valuable to the interests of sports, education, economy, and national defense. The second prizewinner was a paper on ''The Development of an 8-Channel Telemetric Electromyograph System'' that could measure electric signals from eight muscles of an athlete during intense movements. The system provides data greatly facilitating scientific training methods.

The Society is a treasure house of talent. Over the past few years, members of the Society have provided input regarding the formulation of major policies on sports science and technology and put forward suggestions for the 1981-1990 Development Program of Sports Science. The Society is responsible for the compilation of a survey on the *Sports Science Levels of China and Other Countries and the Differences Between Them*, which will be published as the 21st volume of the work *Research Data on China in the Year 2000*. The survey will be of both theoretical and practical value.

Academic Tours and Exchanges

In order to popularize sports science and technology and to disseminate advances in sports research, sports teaching, and training, the Society often sponsors academic tours of the country by Chinese and foreign scholars and experts. It also organizes classes for advanced studies and hosts forums on medical care for the elderly. It has compiled and published two quarterly magazines, *Sports Science* and *Chinese Sports Medical Science*, as well as a popular science journal, *Living Life to the Full*, which has been circulated both at home and abroad.

Great progress has also been made in academic exchanges on national defense sports studies. Over the past few years, some 120 Chinese scientists have attended international academic symposiums on sport psychology, sports biomechanics, sports science of Asian Games, and American and Japanese sports medicine. More than 50 papers have been presented by Chinese participants at these meetings. The Society has also sent people to study scientific research on sports in the United States, Canada, Japan, Switzerland, and the Federal Republic of Germany. It also invited experts from the United States, the Federal Republic of Germany, Austria, and other countries to come to China to present lectures to audiences totaling over 2,000 people. An international scientific event deserving special mention is the Beijing International Conference on Sports Medicine organized by the Chinese Association of Sports Medicine and held November 4-7, 1985. Attending the meetings were 264 specialists and scholars from 17 countries and regions. A total of 262 papers were presented, of which 188 were by Chinese scholars and 74 by foreign participants. The symposium won praise from both Chinese and foreign scholars.

The China Sports Science Society and the China Council for the Promotion of International Trade jointly sponsored an international exhibition of sports equipment and apparatus from June 3-9, 1986. The exhibition attracted more than 70 companies and manufacturers from 11 countries and Hong Kong. More than 1,000 kinds of exhibits represented the advanced level of work in this area and received great praise from both domestic and foreign visitors.

The China Sports Science Society has now been admitted to the International Sports Science and Sports Council as a class A member. Jin Jichun was elected executive member of the council. The Chinese Association of Sports Medicine has joined the International Federation of Sports Medicine (FIMS). Professor Qu Mianyu, president of both the Chinese Association of Sports Medicine and of Beijing Medical University, was elected a vice-president of the Federation in 1986. The China Sports Biomechanics Society has joined the International Sports Biomechanics Society and the International Biomechanics Society. The China Sports Psychology Society has joined the International Sports Psychology Society.

In its 8 years of existence, the China Sports Science Society has proved an effective link between the government and sports science workers. It assists the government in developing sports science and technology and thus plays an important role in the development of physical culture and sports.

Summary

While sports and sports organizations have enjoyed a long history in China, the most extensive developments regarding organizational structure have taken place in the short period since the establishment of the People's Republic of

China in 1949. Contact and exchange with other nations through sport and the emergence of China to a prominent place among major sport nations have required a highly organized structure of sport and physical education administration. In turn, the establishment of an effective organizational structure has resulted in great success from the most basic instructional programs for school children to the highest levels of international competition.

Photo on facing page: Young children in China playing soccer.

Chapter 4

Physical Education in the Schools

QU Zonghu

At the base of the pyramid of sports participation is the instructional program for school children. Governmental authorities recognized early that sound skill, knowledge, and attitude in physical exercise and sport requires organization, management, planning, and implementation based on well-formulated policies.

The Role of Physical Education in Schools

In the 12 years between the entrance to primary school and graduation from middle school, a student in China receives at least 2 hours of physical education course work every week and spends 1 hour each day exercising. This not only develops good physiques, but aids the intellectual and moral development of the nearly 200 million primary and middle school students who represent China's future. The discipline and character developed in physical education helps develop productive citizens who will love the socialist motherland and maintain high ideals.

Goals of Physical Education

Physical well-being helps promote mental development, temper a strong will, and cultivate discipline and good work habits. These qualities are needed to meet the challenges of building a modern China. The intense study necessary to train leaders in science and technology, for example, requires good health. China therefore regards school physical education programs as a key element in the training of talented people and the raising of the country's scientific and technological level. By ensuring a healthy, disciplined populace, physical education also improves the country's industrial and agricultural workforce.

A more direct benefit of physical education programs is the discovery and development of outstanding young athletes. School physical education is the foundation of China's comprehensive sports training system. As such, it has done much to make China an increasingly dominant player in world sports.

Chen Jing, Li Hui, and Jiao Ahimin captured all three medals in women's table tennis at the 1988 Olympic Summer Games in Seoul.

Tasks of Physical Education

The following are specific tasks of school physical education programs.

- *Organizing systematic physical exercises for the improvement of physique.* Exercises bring about coordinated development of the growing human organism, ensure correct carriage, improve the functions of every organ and system in the body, and enhance the ability of the human body to adapt to environmental circumstances.
- *Helping students to master basic knowledge and skills in physical exercise and foster habits of performing exercise on their own.* At the same time, the schools also help students learn the basic aspects of safe living.
- *Conducting moral and aesthetic education, developing the students' intelligence, cultivating good habits, and promoting healthy personalities.* Physical education teaches students to love the socialist motherland, heightens their consciousness of doing exercises for the four modernizations of China (industry, agriculture, defense, and science/technology), and imbues them with the virtues of discipline, unity and friendship, vigor and vitality, and bravery and diligence. The schools help students learn to love, appreciate, and show beauty. The schools also help the students gain self-confidence, independence, creativity, initiative, and other desirable mental and psychological characteristics.

Physical education is designed to encourage physical and mental development, discipline, and unity in Chinese youngsters.

- *Giving systematic part-time training to students with a bright future in sports and helping the state discover excellent athletes.*

Objectives of Physical Education

The following have been identified as specific objectives for the physical education curriculum in the primary grades (1-6):

- Improve the students' health, promote normal physical development, and help them gain a correct carriage.
- Help students to master basic exercise movements and the skills of walking, running, jumping, and hurling; to develop coordination and speed; and to enhance strength and endurance.
- Help foster the students' love of sports.
- Help foster the spirit of unity, friendship, liveliness, initiative, and love of beauty and civilization.

In the junior middle school (grades 7-9) the specific objectives are the following:

- Ensure students' full physical and functional development and the establishment of correct carriage.
- Help students master sports skills.
- Help students learn the importance of physical education and acquire a basic knowledge of sports physiology and hygiene.
- Foster students' love of sports and good exercise habits.
- Help foster students' communist morality and character.

In the senior middle school (grades 10-12), the specific objectives are the following:

- Complete the students' physical growth, consolidate correct carriage, and further improve their physiques and basic functions.
- Teach more about sports theory, foster the idea that good health is a requirement of society, help students master the method of scientific conditioning, expand and improve the sports skills they have learned, and further encourage the development of habits for performing regular exercise in the future.
- Cultivate communist morality, will, character, initiative, and creativity; encourage students to appreciate beauty and good habits.

Organization and Management of Physical Education in Schools

Special commissions, offices, and other agencies both centralized and local have been set up to supervise and administer physical education in the schools.

National Organization

The administrative structure for physical education in the schools of China is presented in Figure 4.1. Two systems control Chinese school physical education. One is the State Education Commission, which is a functionary department directly overseeing all schools through its Department of Physical Culture and Public Health. This agency oversees all matters concerning principles

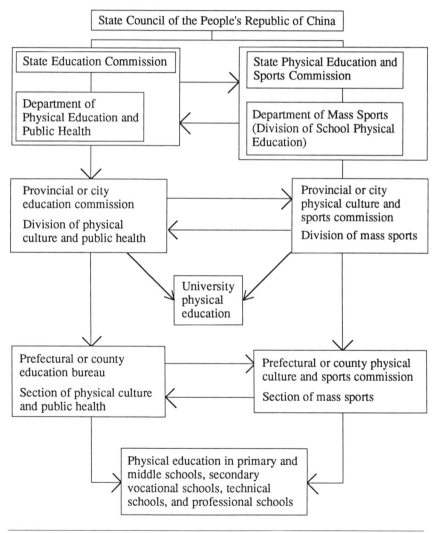

Figure 4.1 Administrative structure for physical education in the public school system of the People's Republic of China.

and policies of physical education in schools. This includes formulating regulations, education plans, teaching curricula, extracurricular training, and school sports competition. A division of physical culture and public health has been set up in each of the provincial education commissions to provide direct leadership to the schools in each particular area.

Assisting the State Education Commission's Department of Physical Culture and Public Health in the administration of school physical education is the State Physical Education and Sports Commission's Division of School Physical Education. It plays a supervisory role in strengthening organizational leadership in areas of mass sports, spare-time training of outstanding athletes in schools, and sports competition.

The State Education Commission and the State Physical Education and Sports Commission coordinate their efforts in leading the country's physical education in schools.

Local Organization

Figure 4.2 illustrates the administrative organization of physical education in a city school system.

The administrative hierarchy that administers physical education of a city has the following tasks:

- It studies and designs the city's plan for developing physical education in the schools and helps implement the plan in accordance with directives from the administrative agencies at higher levels as appropriate to the actual conditions of the locality.
- It gives direct leadership to and administers the schools' physical education work in various districts of the city and gives guidance to or inspects physical education work in outlying districts and townships.
- It gives general leadership to or manages the teaching of mass sports activities and spare-time physical training in schools.
- It develops the actual work plan for physical education, organizes sports contests in primary and middle schools, and recommends outstanding athletes to the sports departments concerned.
- It organizes vocational study and research activities and organizes advanced and continuing education for physical education teachers.
- It organizes scientific study of school physical education.
- It inspects and evaluates the quality of school physical education programs.

The management process starts with investigation and study and proceeds to a continuous cycle of policy-making, implementation, supervision, and feedback. Figure 4.3 shows a diagram of the process.

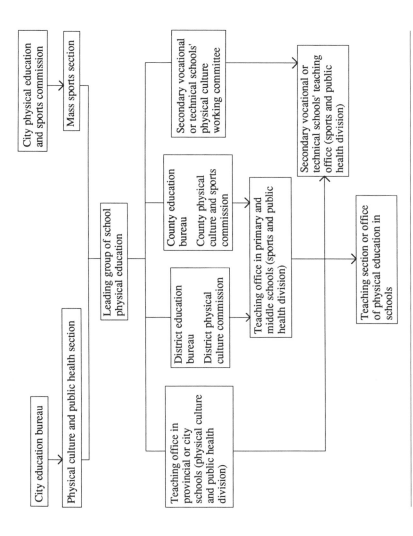

Figure 4.2 Representative model for the administrative organization of physical education in city schools.

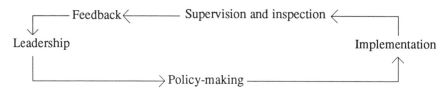

Figure 4.3 The cyclical management process of physical education in Chinese schools.

Regulations Concerning Physical Education in Schools

The state conducts a general management of school physical education mainly through promulgation of education and physical culture decrees and the development of special regulations. The Constitution of the People's Republic of China stipulates that the citizens of the People's Republic of China have the right and obligation to education. The Constitution further requires that the state encourage its youth to develop morally, intellectually, and physically. This is the foundation on which school physical culture policies are made, and all schools must follow this general principle in carrying out physical education.

The former Ministry of Education presented the "Temporary Work Regulations for Schools" in 1963. These regulations were subdivided into "Temporary Work Regulations for All Institutions of Higher Learning in the Country," "Temporary Work Regulations for Full-Time Middle Schools," and "Temporary Work Regulations for Full-Time Primary Schools." The provisions of these documents continue to guide and regulate physical education in China's schools today. They include clear-cut provisions concerning the status and role of school physical education and public health, teaching methods, after-class physical education, equipment and apparatus of school playgrounds, and the administrative management of physical culture and public health in schools. The basic requirements laid down in these provisions serve as standards for inspecting and evaluating a school's physical education and sanitation work.

The State Physical Training Standards, approved by the State Council in July 1982 and jointly published by the State Physical Education and Sports Commission and the State Education Commission in August 1982, are also important guidelines for physical education in the schools. Table 4.1 shows the test events established by the State Physical Training Standards.

The State Physical Training Standards provide a testing system for evaluating both the health of students and the effectiveness of physical education. The standards seek to encourage students' active participation in physical exercise so as to improve their physiques and raise the technical level of sports

Table 4.1 Test Events for the State Physical Training Standards

Category	Age group			
	Children (9-12 years)	Junior 1 (13-15 years)	Junior 2 (16-17 years)	Youth (18 and older)
Type 1	50-m run 25-m shuttle run (10 sec)	50-m run 25-m shuttle run (10 sec)	50-m run 25-m shuttle run (10 sec)	50-m run 100-m run
Type 2	1-min rope skip 400-m run 25-m shuttle run (2 min) 100-m swim 500-m ice-skate	1,000-m run (boys) 1,500-m run (boys) 800-m run (girls) 25-m shuttle run (3 min) 200-m swim	1,000-m run (boys) 1,500-m run (boys) 800-m run (girls) 25-m shuttle run (4 min) 200-m swim 1,000-m ice-skate	1,000-m run (boys) 1,500-m run (boys) 800-m run (girls) 1,500-m ice-skate (boys) 1,000-m ice-skate (girls) 2-000-m swim
Type 3	Long jump High jump Standing long jump	Long jump High jump Standing long jump	Long jump High jump Standing long jump	Long jump High jump Standing long jump
Type 4	Softball throw (25.42 cm circumference) Sandbag throw (0.25 kg)	Medicine ball throw (2 kg) Shot put (3 kg)	Medicine ball throw (2 kg) Shot put (boys—5 kg; girls—4 kg)	Medicine ball throw (2 kg) Shot put (boys—5 kg; girls—4 kg)
Type 5	Pole climbing 1-min situps	Chinups (boys) 1-min situps (girls) Weight lift (boys—15 kg; girls—10 kg)	Chinups (boys) 1-min situps (girls) Weight lift (boys—20 kg; girls—12.5 kg)	Chinups (boys) 1-min situps (girls) Weight lift (boys—20 kg; girls—12.5 kg)

performance. They are also aimed at cultivating the students' moral character and serving better the socialist modernization drive.

The State Physical Training Standards have been implemented in all schools. By 1986, 100 million students had attained or surpassed the standards.

Curriculum and Structure
for Teaching Physical Education

Some countries in Europe established physical education as a required course in schools in the latter part of the 18th century or early in the 19th century. China had a modern school system by 1904 and began to introduce "gymnastic training course" to the school program at that time. This evolved into what was termed a "physical culture course" in 1922. Since its founding in 1949, the People's Republic of China has attached importance to physical education, regarding it as an important part of educational policy.

The chief characteristics of physical training classes are that the students, guided by teachers, carry out physical exercises in an organized and planned way to master physical culture knowledge and skills as well as build up their health. Teachers adopt different materials in their teaching in accordance with the different ages and health conditions of their students.

Table 4.2   Classification of Curriculum Elements and Alotted Percentage of Teaching Hours in Primary Schools

	Grade				
Classification	1	2	3	4	5
Basic curriculum elements					
Basic knowledge of physical culture	6	6	6	6	6
Walking, running, jumping, throwing, and hurling	24	24	22	22	22
Formation, gymnastic formation, basic gymnastics, acrobatic gymnastics, vault with support, and low horizontal bar	24	24	22	22	22
Games	30	30	26	20	20
Wushu (martial arts)	0	0	6	8	8
Selective curriculum elements	16	16	16	20	20
Total percentage of hours	100	100	100	100	100

Physical Education Curriculum

The *Physical Education Curriculum* is a basic document by which the government guides all schools in physical education. Published and circulated by the State Education Commission since 1956, the *Curriculum* constitutes the most important set of guidelines available to physical education teachers. It has been revised twice in 1961 and 1978.

The *Curriculum*'s classification of curriculum elements and distribution of teaching hours among them are presented in Tables 4.2 and 4.3.

The *Curriculum* also stipulates the requirements of examinations. These examinations evaluate several basic components of the students' physical education level. Table 4.4 illustrates these components and the percentage of the

Table 4.3 Middle School Physical Training Content and Alotted Percentage of Teaching Hours

Classification	Grade				
	1	2	3	4	5
Basic curriculum elements					
Basic knowledge of physical culture	6	6	6	6	6
Walking, running, jumping, throwing, and hurling	26	28	28	28	28
Formation, basic gymnastics, acrobatic gymnastics, vault with support, horizontal bar, and parallel bars	26	24	24	18	18
Ball games	14	14	14	12	12
Wushu	8	8	8	6	6
Selective curriculum elements	20	20	20	30	30
Total percentage of hours	100	100	100	100	100

Table 4.4 Content of Evaluation and Percentage of Scores

Content	Percentage of score (%)
In-class performance	10
Knowledge of physical culture	20
Sports skills	30
Physique	40

total score represented by each one. The scores are derived by comparing individual students' performances to the State Physical Training Standards (see Table 4.1).

Class Structure and Teaching Plans

Physical education teachers organize instruction for each year and each class in accordance with the curriculum guidelines published by the government. All curricula involve at least 2 hours of instruction per week.

Students are required to perform physical exercises so as to increase physiologic capacity. Teachers must not only follow general principles of learning but must also pay particular attention to the changes in physiological functions students undergo through growth and exercise. When a human body enters into an active state from a sedentary state, its functional power always moves from a lower level gradually to a higher level and then to a lower level again. This law of "rise—stability—fall" reflects the physiological responses to exercise for the individual. Following this law, physical education classes

Physical education classes play an important role in the selection process used to identify sports potential.

are divided into three parts: preparation, main exercises, and conclusion. These parts are closely related and form a complete process. The content, organizing work, and time allocated to each part may vary according to special features of the students, available facilities, and weather conditions in different seasons. The class structure varies from time to time. At present, teachers in many provinces and cities are studying ways to revise and improve physical education class structure.

In general, teachers take the following steps in devising a teaching plan:

- Devise a plan for the whole school year: Components and hours are divided reasonably into two semesters. Teaching hours, activities, and standards for examination for each teaching material are then fixed.
- Devise a semester schedule: Content of each semester is arranged in accordance with the teaching plan for the whole year.
- Devise a unit plan: The total hours for each curriculum element are regarded as a unit for which concrete time requirements are determined. The time to be devoted to each unit is adjusted according to its importance to the overall program.
- Devise a plan for teaching hours: Concrete tasks, content, organizations, teaching steps, and amount of exercise are fixed in accordance with the unit plans.

Spare-Time Sports Activities in the Primary and Middle Schools

In China, the school physical education class is the chief form of physical education in the primary and middle schools. Other forms during the school hours are the morning exercises performed at the start of the day and exercise during the morning break. Also there are after-school group exercises, school games, and free sport activities, all of which are referred to as spare-time sports activities.

It is necessary to encourage and organize the students to join these spare-time sports activities to ensure adequate total time for physical exercise. This not only strengthens the students' physiques and enriches their cultural life, but also helps them develop good habits of physical exercise.

Morning Exercises and Exercises During Class Breaks

Every student in China is expected to take part in the morning exercises or in exercises during the class break. Morning exercises are conducted in the early morning or just before class begins. Students who are boarding at schools must spend 15 to 20 minutes every morning performing each exercise. Other students exercise for 10 to 15 minutes before the first class begins. Students may also participate in calisthenics or take part in jogging or simple exercises.

Exercises during the class break take place between the second and third class hours in the morning. Such exercises help get rid of the students' fatigue after their strenuous study and give their brains a chance to rest. They also help prevent students from adopting an incorrect carriage. Besides performing "radio calisthenics" (exercise sessions led by program broadcast by Chinese radio stations) during the class break, the students can also perform exercises aimed at preventing poor posture, jog, or play games.

After-School Exercises

After class, the students in primary and middle schools are organized to perform physical training of various kinds in accordance with their gender, health condition, and interests. Training teams and groups are formed, each consisting of 10 to 15 students on the average.

Each team carries out physical training for an hour at least twice a week. To ensure that the students exercise every day, these spare-time physical training periods are usually set on days when students have no physical education classes.

Activities for spare-time physical training are specified in the State Physical Training Standards. Students can also review and consolidate the basic

Spare-time physical training after school provides additional opportunity for skill development.

materials they have learned in their physical education classes or take part in swimming, skating, and other sports contests, according to the season of the year.

Spare-time physical training plays an important role in meeting the needs of the students for physical exercise and developing sports skills.

School Games

Various sports contests are held during holidays or after school in almost all primary and middle schools in China. Track-and-field contests are common and are usually held in the spring and autumn.

Games serve as a comprehensive review of a school's physical education and achievements in teaching and training. They promote a school's mass sports activities and raise the level of sports participation. They cultivate the students' discipline, collective spirit, and sense of honor. They also stimulate the teachers and the students and generally enliven the students' lives.

School sports games in China started in 1890, when St. John's College in Shanghai organized games with track-and-field activities as the major competitive events. Later, such games spread to middle schools and other universities in large cities. Since the founding of the People's Republic of China, sports games have been held in both town and country schools. The games have become a traditional activity and an important part of education in schools.

School games take forms other than track-and-field events. For example, competition is common in basketball, volleyball, soccer, table tennis, and badminton. In the lower grades, competition is frequently held in rope jumping, elastic rope skipping (termed Chinese jumprope in the United States), and other simple events.

Free Sports Activities

Students may train in one or several sports according to their personal likings. Such activities are not compulsory and the students may choose them without outside pressure.

Free physical training usually takes place during class breaks, after classes, or on holidays. Such training commonly includes rope skipping, elastic rope skipping, kicking the shuttlecock, and informal games. Such activities enrich the students' lives and are beneficial to their physical and mental growth.

Summary

Governmental and educational authorities have expended great effort to identify goals and objectives that contribute to the aims of contemporary Chinese society and are compatible with the country's political system. Because a unified educational system serves the children of China, every child is provided with a program in which central planning and administration assures content and quality.

Chapter 5

Preparation of Physical Education Teachers

QU Zonghu

Physical education teachers are the actual organizers and executors of physical education in schools. Therefore, the training and preparation of enough well-qualified physical education teachers represents one of the major tasks in realizing the goals of physical education in schools.

Current Supply of Physical Education Teachers

Most of the physical education institutions that existed before the Socialist revolution were small in scale and short in longevity. Incomplete statistics suggest that the physical education institutions of all kinds in this country produced a total of about 10,000 graduates from the late Qing Dynasty through 1949, the year the People's Republic of China was founded.

Since the founding of New China, the number of physical education teachers in Chinese schools has undergone constant expansion. These teachers have contributed immeasurably to the development of physical education. The tremendous number of school-age children and the rapid development of education, however, have proved to be far more than the existing contingent can bear in terms of both quantity and quality. Table 5.1 shows the results of a study conducted by the State Education Commission regarding the present status of physical education teachers in secondary and primary schools.

Obviously the training and preparation of enough well qualified physical education teachers is a very urgent and arduous task. The State Education Commission has made it a rule that physical education teachers in primary, junior middle, and senior middle schools are expected to have an educational background equivalent to a secondary normal school diploma, a college associate diploma, and an undergraduate diploma, respectively. It is estimated that by the year 2000, 470,000 more secondary and primary physical education teachers will be needed and 120,000 present teachers will require more advanced education. This is a challenging task, but measures are being taken to expand the number of teachers and raise the quality of teaching. To encourage interest in the field, physical education teachers are granted the same status and treatment as teachers in all other fields. Successful teachers are awarded titles of "Outstanding Teacher" or "Special-Grade Teacher." Some of them can be elected deputies to the National People's Congress and/or the People's

Table 5.1 Physical Education Teachers for Primary and Secondary Schools

Type of school	Hiring quotas	Number of available teachers	Number of vacancies	Percentage of available teachers that are certified
Primary	340,000	40,000	300,000	25.0
Junior middle	143,000	93,000	50,000	18.6
Senior middle	37,000	27,000	10,000	24.6
Total	520,000	160,000	360,000	21.9

Political Consultative Conference. Holiday tours and vacations are also enjoyed by those who have done outstanding jobs.

To ensure competent teaching, the government established criteria regarding care of students, dedication to the profession, willingness to serve the people and the educational course, sufficient academic background, and good health. In 1987, a qualification certificate program was implemented to help raise the quality of all teachers, including those in physical education.

Training Options for Physical Education Teachers

In order to meet the demand imposed by such a large school population, additional training institutions were created and various pathways provided for teacher training. The various options provided have helped immeasurably in meeting this demand.

Physical Education Institutes

To keep up with the development of Chinese education and meet its need for physical education teachers, a number of physical education institutes have been established since the founding of New China (see Table 5.2). November 8, 1952, saw the establishment of the first institute of this kind in New China—the

The Shanghai Institute of Physical Education is one of fourteen institutes where physical education teachers are trained.

Table 5.2   Six Physical Education Institutes Directly Under the State Physical Education and Sports Commission (1987)

Institute	Faculty			Enrollment	Area (hectares)	Sports played in gymnasiums	Sports played outdoors	Supplemental facilities
	Total staff	Professors and associate professors	Lecturers					
Beijing	581	191	278	2,354	60	Track-and-field Swimming Gymnastics Rhythmics Wushu Table tennis Weight lifting Wrestling Ball games	Track-and-field Ball games Archery Swimming	Library Computer room Media center Anatomy lab Research center
Shanghai	300	94	138	979	30.5	Track-and-field Gymnastics Ball games Wushu	Track-and-field Ball games	Anatomy lab Biological research center

Wuhan	282	85	113	1,237	43.4	Track-and-field Gymnastics Ball games Comprehensive facility	Track-and-field Ball games	Research center
Chengdu	210	76	103	1,418	11	Ball games Gymnastics Rhythmics Table tennis	Track-and-field Ball games	Library Teaching laboratory
Shenyang	208	71	98	946	10.7	Track-and-field Gymnastics Ball games Table tennis	Track-and-field Ball games	Library Research center
Xi'an	222	62	65	1,302	20.7	Ball games Gymnastics	Track-and-field Gymnastics Ball games	Library

East China Institute of Physical Education, later renamed the Shanghai Institute of Physical Education. In 1953 the Central Institute of Physical Education (now known as the Beijing Institute of Physical Education) was established. As of 1986, there were 14 physical education institutes—Beijing, Shanghai, Wuhan, Shenyang, Xi'an, Chengdu, Tianjin, Guangzhou, Harbin, Jilin, Shandong, Nanjing, Fujian, and Hebei. Table 5.2 presents information about the six institutes that are directly under the State Commission of Physical Culture and Sports.

During the past three decades, over 60,000 students have obtained undergraduate diplomas or associate diplomas from the 14 institutes. Students study from a large offering of courses. The academic units and the courses offered by the various departments of these institutes are as follows:

Departments of Physical Education: These departments train teachers for secondary schools and other physical education professionals. Admission is granted to graduates of secondary schools or other young people with equivalent qualifications. Students in these departments undertake a 4-year course. A 2-year course may also be possible for students who want to be teachers in junior middle schools.

Departments of Sports: With the training and preparation of sports coaches and instructors as their main goal, these departments recruit secondary school graduates (or equivalents) to follow a 4-year course. Priority is given to applicants with demonstrated skill in a particular sport. Each student pursues a certain sport as a major area of study, such as track-and-field, gymnastics, basketball, volleyball, football, table tennis, swimming, or wushu.

Departments of Sports Science: Courses are offered in fields related to sports science, for example, anatomy of motion, physiology of exercise, sports medicine, biomechanics of sport, and sports biochemistry. Students are trained to be teachers of sports science. Entrants are secondary school graduates or their equivalents. Except for sports medicine, which is a 5-year course, all courses of study offered in these departments last 4 years.

Graduate Schools: Graduate schools mainly train physical education teachers for colleges and universities, coaches, and sports scientists. Applicants must have successfully completed an undergraduate course or have equivalent qualification. Courses last 2 to 3 years. Those who complete a 3-year course receive a master's degree when they pass the degree examination and thesis defense.

Departments of In-Service Training: Short-term courses are offered to meet the needs of physical education teachers, coaches, and administrators who want to improve their competence.

Departments of Corresponding Courses: Most of the students who follow correspondence courses are on-the-job teachers, coaches, and physical education personnel qualified for secondary school teaching.

Sports Schools: These schools train potential elite athletes and provide the other physical education institutes with qualified applicants.

Physical Education Departments in Multi-Disciplinary Colleges and Universities

In addition to specialized physical education institutes, there are 116 physical education departments in comprehensive colleges and universities. There is also a Teachers College of Physical Education in Beijing. In addition, the Physical Education Department of the Beijing Teachers University produced 967 graduates between 1959 and 1983. Physical education teachers are also trained in schools for secondary teachers.

Continuing Education of Teachers

According to the qualification certificate program, approximately 125,000 physical education teachers in secondary and primary schools will receive

Young soccer players learn basic skills from a master teacher.

continuing education, ranging from a summer of study to a few years. A number of forms and approaches have been adopted to fulfill this goal. Such teachers have several options.

- They may take advanced courses in physical education institutes or departments to refresh their knowledge, improve their sports skills, and increase teaching ability. Some can obtain degrees as a result of successful completion.
- They may study in colleges (or schools) of advanced pedagogy on either a full-time or a part-time basis.
- They may take correspondence courses. Degrees are awarded to those who pass relevant examinations.
- They may attend training camps during vacations.
- They may participate in activities such as seminars or demonstrations or evaluations organized by local teaching and study centers in which experiences and opinions can be exchanged and competence improved.
- They may follow educational television programs.

Basic Requirements in Physical Education Programs

Educational programs, the guiding documents laid out by the government, reflect the unified requirements for teaching in schools and colleges. They provide an important basis for the implementation of educational programs in schools and colleges. So that both consistency and flexibility can be maintained, physical education institutes may formulate their own educational programs considering both the country's unified requirements and their own needs and possibilities.

Curricula

The Beijing Institute of Physical Education illustrates the pattern of curricula to which the other institutes adhere. The aim of the Beijing Institute is to train physical education teachers and other specialists who are both dedicated and competent. Subjects are grouped into three categories: compulsory subjects, selective subjects, and free elective subjects. Students are obliged to complete prescribed units of credits within each of these three categories as well as additional units for field work and thesis requirements. In the field of sports skills, students are required to specialize in one sport. At the completion of their major studies, students are encouraged to select a minor either in an academic field (e.g., physiology of exercise or sport psychology) or in another sport. The following is a list of available subjects within each of the three categories.

1. **Compulsory Subjects** (Number in brackets indicates number of class hours)

History of the Chinese Communist Party	(72)
Philosophy	(72)
Political Economy	(72)
Introduction to Physical Education	(24)
Pedagogy	(72)
Sport Psychology	(72)
Sports Medicine	(72)
Biochemistry of Sport	(50)
History of Sports and Physical Education in China	(48)
Physical Education in Schools	(54)
Anatomy of Motion I	(72)
Physiology of Exercise I	(108)
Biomechanics of Sport	(72)
Statistics in Physical Education	(54)
Foreign Language	(288)
Track-and-Field	(216)
Gymnastics	(216)
Basketball	(72)
Volleyball	(72)
Soccer (male students)	(72)
Rhythmics (female students)	(72)
Swimming	(72)
Wushu	(72)
Weight Lifting	(36)
Major Sport	(432)
Major Study	(328)
Research Project and Graduation Thesis	(164)

2. **Selective Subjects** (Each student is required to complete six selective subject credit units; the second number in the parentheses indicates units of credits)

Sport Training	(36, 2)
Mass Sports	(24, 1)
Physical Therapy	(36, 2)
Measurements and Evaluation in Physical Education	(72, 4)
Computer Languages	(54, 3)

3. **Free Electives** (Each student is required to complete six credit units; number in parentheses indicates units of credit)

Philosophy of Sports	(2)

Logic	(2)
Economy of Sports	(2)
Aesthetics of Sports	(2)
Basic Cybernetics in Sports	(2)
Introduction to Decision Making in Sports	(2)
Laws and Regulations in Sports	(2)
Ethics of Sports	(2)
History of World Sports	(2)
Higher Mathematics	(4)
Basic Writing Skills	(4)
Written Communication	(4)
Selected Reading of Classic Chinese Literature	(4)
Advanced Foreign Language	(8)
Technical English	(8)
Study and Practice of Foreign Languages	(4)
Anatomy of Motion II	(4)
Morphology of Motion	(1)
Physiology of Exercise II	(4)
Physiology of Human Adaptation	(1)
Biochemistry of Sport	(3)
Sports Injuries	(2)
Medical Monitoring in Sports	(2)
Nutrition and Hygiene	(1)
Applications of Electronic Devices in Sports	(2)
Fine Arts	(2)
Music	(2)
Daoyin Exercises	(1)
Table Tennis	(2)
Badminton	(1)
Tennis	(1)
Handball	(1)
Baseball and Softball	(1)
Bowling and Gate Ball (croquet)	(1)
Women's Soccer	(1)
Rhythmics II	(2)
Calisthenics	(2)
Mass Games	(1)
Roller Skating	(1)

Water Polo	(1)
Skin Diving	(1)
Synchronized Swimming	(1)
Taijiquan and Taiji Sword	(2)
Wrestling	(1)
Fitness and Strength	(1)
Fencing	(1)
Gymnastics II	(2)
Games and Play	(1)

Practice Teaching

Upon completion of the prescribed units of credit for their particular educational programs, students must do field work, which is normally undertaken during the eighth semester of study. Students spend 8 to 10 weeks engaged in practice teaching in a secondary school. At the end of the field work, which is done under the auspices of a supervisor, comments and evaluations will be given to the practice teacher. Satisfactory completion of field work is one of the prerequisites for graduation.

In field work, students apply the knowledge and skills they have gained. Teaching physical education classes is the major part of field work. Other activities include organizing sports meets and extracurricular activities, training

Field work offers student teachers opportunities to apply their knowledge and skills.

school teams, and taking responsibility for a class group. Through practice teaching, students develop a better understanding of physical education in secondary schools and a basic mastery of teaching methods and approaches. This greatly benefits the students because they will be assigned jobs in secondary schools upon graduation and will be able to adapt to these job assignments more smoothly.

Staff in Physical Education Institutes

The quality of school physical education programs depends greatly upon the quality of teachers. The quality of physical education teaching personnel depends, in turn, upon the quality of the faculty of the institutes where they are trained.

Present Status

Along with the development of physical education in higher education in the New China, the ranks of teachers in physical education institutes have been growing steadily. In 1954, there were more than 300 full-time teachers in six physical education institutes (Central, East China, Midsouth China, Southwest China, Northwest China, and Northeast China), which are now called the Beijing, Shanghai, Wuhan, Chengdu, Xi'an, and Shenyang Institutes of Physical Education, respectively. By 1983, there were more than 2,800 teachers, an eightfold increase over 1954. Among this number, there were 25 professors, 270 associate professors, and 1,237 lecturers. Of all the physical education institutes in China, the Beijing Institute of Physical Education has the largest and strongest staff, including 7 professors, 70 associate professors, 278 lecturers, 104 tutors, and 122 non-ranked teachers (as of 1986).

Following in the footsteps of such outstanding experts as Wu Yunrui, Xu Yingchao, Zhang Huilan, Zheng Haixian, Ma Qiwei, and Wang Yirun, a large number of young and middle-aged teachers with solid academic qualification and eagerness to bring forth new ideas have emerged into roles of leadership in the physical education institutes. Many of them have received postgraduate education or have been further educated overseas. Some of them have obtained master's and doctoral degrees and have the titles of professor, associate professor, or lecturer. Graduate students are the main source of teachers in physical education institutes.

Graduate Study Programs

Much has been achieved in the training of graduate students in an attempt to produce more advanced physical education professionals. Over the past three decades, more than 500 graduate students have been trained in physical education institutes.

In late 1981, the State Council approved master's degree programs offered by the Beijing Institute of Physical Education in Theory of Sports and Physical Education, Human Physiology, Theory and Methods of Teaching Physical Activities, and Sports Training. At the same time, the Shanghai Institute of Physical Education received approval for master's programs in Theory of Sports and Physical Education, Human Anatomy, and Human Physiology. In 1982, the National Commission for Academic Degrees empowered the eight physical education institutes at Beijing, Shanghai, Wuhan, Shenyang, Xi'an, Chengdu, Tianjin, and Guangzhou to offer bachelor's degrees. In 1986, accreditation was granted to the Beijing Institute of Physical Education in Physiology of Exercise and Volleyball and to the Shanghai Institute of Physical Education for a doctoral program in Theory of Sports and Physical Education. This represented a new stage in the training of graduate students.

Graduate studies are run on a credit basis. With the help of their instructors, graduate students select the required subjects according to their major interest and specialities. Of the selected subjects, two or three must be in the area of sports science. The following is a listing of subjects available to graduate students at the Beijing Institute of Physical Education (number in brackets indicates units of credit).

1. Compulsory Subjects

Dialectics of Nature	(4)
Foreign Language	(8)
Major Study	(12)

2. Elective Subjects

Experiments in Physiology of Exercise	(3)
Sport Psychology and Experiments	(2)
Biomechanics of Sport	(2)
Experiments in Biomechanics	(2)
Experiments in Biochemistry	(2)
Nutrition and Hygiene	(1)
Physical Therapy	(1)
Sports Injuries	(2)
Medical Monitoring	(2)
Multifactor Analysis	(2)
Experiment Design in Statistics	(2)
Measurements and Evaluation in Physical Education	(2)
Higher Mathematics	(4)
Theoretical Mechanics	(2)

Applied Mathematics	(1)
Pedagogy	(2)
Sports Training	(2)
Logic	(2)
Three Basic Scientific Approaches	(1)
Indexing and Cataloging of Sports Literature	(1)
Demonstrations of Sports Skills (Track, Gymnastics)	(4)
Biocybernetics	(1)
Computer Languages	(2)

Graduate students are also required to undertake field work. Those who pursue a 3-year course must complete a research thesis defense to receive the degrees.

Summary

The State Education Commission and the Chinese government have recognized that sound physical education programs require highly competent teachers. To this end, the Commission and the government have encouraged the creation of new departments and institutes and the expansion of established departments and institutes. Thus, the quality of physical education for each generation of physical education teachers has continually improved.

Photo on facing page: A champion athlete, Zheng Dazhen established an Asian record for the women's high jump in 1980.

Chapter 6

Traditional and Popular Sports

WANG Zeshan

The present selection of sports practiced among all age groups in China blends activities rooted in ancient China with activities developed internationally during the last century. These separated strands exist side-by-side as integral parts of contemporary Chinese culture.

Traditional Sports

Whether one studies the physical activities of a school yard or university campus during a school day, or observes adult sport involvement during the early morning hours, one will see exercise and sport routines that have been practiced in China for centuries. These activities play an important role in the daily life of China and are an important aspect of Chinese culture.

Philosophy and Characteristics of Traditional Sports

Traditional Chinese attitudes toward health enhancement differ markedly from those of the West. These attitudes are one of the main reasons that traditional Chinese sports are so distinctive and so different from traditional Western sports events.

Starting with the early development of physical training in China, it can be seen that the activities of traditional Chinese sports are characterized by the following features:

- They have health improvement as their common purpose.
- Their movements often mimic those of living things.
- They embody philosophical concepts of research value.
- Their development reflects that of society.

The orientation of good health practices and health building sports are outstanding components of China's splendid culture. In a sense, this cultural wealth constitutes one of the important factors upon which the whole Chinese nation has relied for existence and development.

Traditional Chinese exercises like taijiquan (shadow boxing), qigong (breathing exercise), wuqinxi (five-animal exercise), baduanjing (eight part exercise), and liangong shibafa (eighteen exercises of martial arts) emphasize *jinggong* (composed exercise), *neigong* (internal exercise), *daoying* (breathing and physical exercise), and the training of *jing* (essence of life), *qi* (vital energy), and *shen* (mental faculties). Additionally, all stress the integration of spirit with appearance, composure with movement, and interior with exterior. This harmonic approach to exercise seeks to unify the efforts of mind, body, and spirit and thereby improve them all.

Historical Development of Traditional Sports

The relationship of exercise to good health was not explicitly recognized in China until the end of the Shang Dynasty (1600-1066 B.C.). Until then, personal health was not given the attention it deserved, and there was little significant development of sports.

During the Western Zhou Dynasty (1066-771 B.C.), however, a growing consciousness of the importance of health maintenance led to the introduction of the Six Arts—ceremony, music, archery, driving, calligraphy, and mathematics—as subjects in school education. During the Spring and Autumn period (770-476 B.C.), Confucius adopted the Six Arts as the course of study and theme of his teaching in his private school. The growing emphasis on health and longevity also led to the development of the ancient exercise *daoying*. Daoying budded during the Western Zhou Period (1066-771 B.C.).

Around A.D. 208, the noted surgeon Hua Tuo, of the late Han Dynasty, devised and compiled Wuqinxi (Five-Animal Play) by summing up the experiences of his predecessors. He also wrote a book, *Wuqinxi*, which was found among the ancient books of the Han Dynasty excavated in 1973 at Mawangdui of Changsha, Hunan province. The book consists of two monographs, one devoted to Daoying exercise and the other an "Atlas of Daoying" containing more than 40 illustrations of various postures of the exercise.

The Ming Dynasty (A.D. 1368-1644) witnessed a further development of the ancient art of wushu in China. Various schools emphasizing different routines and skills took shape during this period. Two of the schools were the Shaolin School (Shaolin shadow boxing) and the Wudang School (Wudang shadow boxing).

Beginning during the latter part of the Ming Dynasty, taijiquan, a new form of China's old-style boxing, came into being. During the Qing Dynasty (A.D. 1644-1911) taijiquan became more and more popular.

In the latter half of the 19th century, Western sports were introduced into China. Many of these sports have since been developed extensively and have contributed to the incorporation of western-style physical training and athletic competition into traditional Chinese sports.

Traditional Health-Building Sports

Since the recognition of the link between health and exercise, many health-improvement and health-maintenance activities have evolved. Several of these sports continue to be popular in China today.

Wushu

Wushu, also called guoshu (national martial arts) and wuyi (skills in martial arts), is one of the most important traditional Chinese sports. Wushu consists of a variety of boxing routines and leg movements. The performance of each movement stresses both bursts of force and softness. Characterized by a wide scope of joint movements, wushu greatly improves the strength and flexibility of muscles and ligaments.

Wushu incorporates, in accordance with standardized rules, kicking, striking, throwing, seizing, tumbling, and other movements into a duel that might be conducted either with or without weapons. According to incomplete statistics, the types of boxing prevailing now in different areas of China and among various nationality groups number well over a thousand. Some of them are divided into a variety of schools.

Geographically, there are the South Boxing School and the North Boxing School. Named for the mountains where they originated, there are the Shaolin

School, the Wudang School, and the Emei School. Classified by their features, there are the Neijia (Neijei shadow boxing) School and the Waijia (Waijia shadow boxing) School. Divided by their technical forms, there are the Changquan (long boxing) School and the Duanquan (short boxing) School. The weapons used in wushu include sabres, swords, spears, halberds, staves, hammers, chains, and maces. Today, wushu is generally classified into five categories:

- Barehanded boxing.
- Practice with weapons (developed from ancient arms).
- Training in pairs, barehanded against barehanded; weapons against weapons; or barehanded against weapons. Offensive and defensive exercises are conducted in set routines between more than two persons.
- Group exhibition performed by six or more persons, with or without weapons.
- Offensive and defensive practice carried out between two persons according to set regulations, freehanded or using hand push (engaging in a push-pull motion and using no weapons) or using short or long weapons.

Exhibition and competition are the main forms of evaluation of wushu skills. The aim is to exchange experiences, improve teaching and training, develop the activity itself, and raise the standards of performance. Usually, the exhibition and competition are conducted on a flat surface 14 meters long and 8 meters wide. As for the use of sabres, spears, swords, and staves in competition, there are set rules and regulations with criteria for scoring. The highest possible score for any event of wushu competition or exhibition is 10. A referee grades each competitor according to the technique and skill displayed.

Qigong

Qigong, or neigong, has a history of more than 3,000 years in China. It is an activity for strengthening the vital energy and a means of maintaining good health.

Qigong can be divided into *jinggong* (composed exercise) and *donggong* (moving exercise). They were so named because, in practice, the former does not exhibit noticeable movement, whereas the latter does.

Qigong is especially effective in improving the function of higher nerve centers. Qigong trains the mental faculties and enhances interaction of the mind and the body. It is also thought to improve the function of the cerebrum. The exercise is believed to prevent illness, delay ageing, and regulate cardiac function.

Qigong has an effect similar to that of massage on the viscera of the abdominal cavity. With practice, the extent of movement of the diaphragm increases three- to fourfold. Qigong's rhythmic and extensive movements also promote peristalsis of the stomach and intestines, alleviate stasis in the abdominal cavity, and enhance digestion and respiration.

Taijiquan

Taijiquan, a form of Chinese boxing, was developed during the late Ming Dynasty and the early Qing Dynasty (A.D. 1368-1800). According to textual research undertaken by Tang Hao (a scholar of China's wushu history) and others, taijiquan was originally practiced by members of a family named Chen in the village of Chenjiagou, Wenxian county, Henan province. The founder of Chen-style boxing was Chen Wangtien, a sagacious wushu master. Taijiquan was developed by incorporating boxing skills of the well known boxers in the Ming Dynasty, integrating ancient daoying with *tuna* (inspiration and expiration exercise), and utilizing the theories of yin and yang from traditional Chinese medicine.

Through the years, taijiquan has become divided into various schools. Among the most popular and distinctive are the Chen-Style, the Yang-Style, the Wu-Style, and the Sun-Style. Although they differ from each other in styles and postures, the structures of their routines and the sequence of their movements are basically the same.

In taijiquan, it is imperative that the posture of every part of the body be not only correct but relaxed, gentle, and natural, so that a portion of the cerebral

Taijiquan exercises require concentration and disciplined movements.

cortex will enter a state of protective inhibition and cease functioning. Taijiquan is believed to have a positive effect on a person's mood and to modify the function of the cerebrum. These relaxed, gentle exercises are thought to facilitate the flow of energy, increase metabolism, and strengthen the physique of even the elderly and the weak.

Wuqinxi

Wuqinxi (five-animal exercise), also called wujin qigong, is a health-building exercise designed originally by the aforementioned surgeon, Hua Tuo. It imitates the shape and movements of five kinds of animals, namely the tiger, the deer, the bear, the ape, and the bird (Figure 6.1).

图 1   五禽戏动作 　图 2   五禽戏动作 　图 3   五禽戏动作
之一——虎寻食 　　之二——鹿长跑 　　之三——熊撼运

图 4   五禽戏动作
之四——猿摘果 　　图 5   五禽戏动作之五——鹤飞翔

Figure 6.1 In Wuqinxi, the five-animal exercise, participants initiate the movements of a prowling tiger, a running deer, a stumbling bear, a foraging ape, and a flying crane.

Traditional Activities Now Performed for Recreation and at Festivals

The people of China as well as Chinese who have emigrated to countries around the world enjoy characteristically Chinese holidays and traditional activities. Though these traditional activities can stand alone, many are regularly included in the program of events for special holidays.

Dragon-Boat Regattas

Usually, dragon-boat regattas are held on the occasion of festivals. The history of this activity is very long. Tradition has it that the first dragon-boat regatta was held in memory of Qu Yuan, a great poet of the Warring States period (475-221 B.C.) who drowned himself in the Miluo River in Hunan province.

Dragon boats are generally 20 to 30 meters long, accommodating about 30 paddlers. They race over a fixed distance, with the first boat across the finish line the winner. During the Han Dynasty (206 B.C.-A.D. 220), dragon-boat regattas were held at annual Dragon-Boat Festivals, which occurred during

Competitors prepare for a dragon-boat race on a national holiday.

the fifth day of the fifth lunar month. Similar activities are carried out by the Miao and Tai people in the southwestern areas of China.

Dragon Dance

Dragon dance, also called dragon lantern or dancing of the dragon, is a traditional folk sport and dance. Ordinarily, the dragon is made of bamboo, wood, paper, and cloth, and is carried in connected sections on the bodies of the dancers. The number of sections of the dragon is not fixed but has to be odd. Each section, or dragon lantern, is lit by a candle. To play with the dragon, a person runs in front and waves a colored ball to tease the dragon one way or another.

The dragon dance dates back to the time of the Han Dynasty (206 B.C.-A.D. 220). At that time, people used dragons to pray for rain using a different dragon in each of the four seasons. In spring they danced with a green dragon, in summer a red dragon, in autumn a white dragon, and in winter a black dragon. By the time of the Song Dynasty (A.D. 960-1279), dragon dancing had become a festive recreational activity. It has been a popular form of dance among the people ever since.

Kite Flying

Kite flying in China has a history of more than 2,000 years. It remains very popular among the masses. Necessarily an outdoor activity, kite flying is often used as recreational therapy.

The traditional kite is made of fine bamboo and thin tissue paper. It is often designed after patterns of various animals such as centipedes, hawks, dragons, butterflies, flying swallows, and fish. Sometimes a kite is made in the form of a figure or an airplane. The kite that flies high, moves lithely, and looks beautiful is considered good.

In recent years, kite flying has been taken up in some places as a competitive event. In 1984, an international kite-flying fair, the first of its kind, was held in Weifang, Shandong province. Participating in the activity were teams and groups from 11 countries and regions.

Horse Racing

Horse racing has a long history in China. It is especially popular in regions inhabited by minority nationalities such as Inner Mongolia, Tibet, Yunnan, and Guizhou. Early in the Spring and Autumn period (770-476 B.C.) and the Warring States period (475-221 B.C.), records were already available on this activity. Handed down from generation to generation, horse racing was gradually popularized.

As customs of the various nationalities differ, horse racing in different regions varies greatly in general format and in the rules of competition. For example, the annual Nadam Fair in Inner Mongolia features horse racing. The people of the Miao nationality race yearly on the eighth day of the fourth lunar month and at the Eighth Month Reed-Pipe Wind Instrument Play Fair. Xui people usually include horse racing on the occasion of their Dragon-Boat Festival. The number of participants in these horse-racing events sometimes reaches a thousand.

Tug-of-War

This activity has a long history in China, being practiced since the Tang Dynasty (A.D. 618-907). Tug-of-war is an athletic contest between two teams composed of an equal number of participants. In order to determine victory and defeat, two parallel lines are drawn on the ground at a fixed distance to serve as the banks of a "river." Across the river a rope is placed. The two teams, one on each side, pull against each other at the opposite ends of the rope. The winner is the team that draws the mark—a red cloth attached to the middle of the rope—over to its side of the river.

These women are competing in a friendly tug-of-war game, an activity originally developed for soldiers preparing for combat in ancient times.

Nadam

This is a favorite traditional event among the Mongolian people of China. In the early days, the Nadam was held among the tribes in July and August every year. Its aim was to promote unity and friendship among the tribes as well as to celebrate harvests. It was also designed to prevent disputes arising from misunderstandings among the tribes regarding the distribution of pastures. The event consists mainly of wrestling, horse racing, and archery but the people of Inner Mongolia refer to the entire occasion as Nadam.

Popular Sports

The term *popular sports* in China generally refers to sports carried out as mass activity. (In other countries, the terms public sports and social sports have been used.) Varied in form and rich in content, popular sports are taken up by staff members and workers in factories, mines, commercial enterprises, institutions, and government organizations, as well as by residents in the cities and towns and farmers in the countryside. The objectives of the participants include health enhancement, recreation, fitness, and the cure of ailments.

Reasons for Governmental Attention to Sports

Since the founding of New China, the government has paid great attention to developing popular sports. Article 21 of the Constitution of China stipulates: ''The State develops physical culture, promotes mass sports and builds up people's physique.'' China's seventh 5-Year Plan promises in explicit terms ''to further raise the standards of every event of sports and strengthen people's constitution on the bases of widely developing popular sports activities.'' Popular sports continue to significantly impact several areas of government concern.

Facilitating Modernization

Modernization requires people not only to master contemporary scientific knowledge and familiarize themselves with up-to-date techniques, but also to have powerful physiques. Popular sports provide an effective way to meet these requirements.

Since the early 1930s, China has promoted work-break exercises among the staff members and workers. Long-term study has shown that this activity helps improve physiologic function, relieves fatigue, and raises productivity.

A survey conducted by a research institute among the staff members and workers in several industrial districts of Shanghai revealed that, of the persons polled, 22.9 percent were found to be suffering from the occupational strain of functional back injury. To alleviate the problem, the Medico-Athletics

Section of the Shanghai Second Medical College and the Nanyang Hospital of the Luwan District jointly devised a set of production exercises for control and treatment of this disorder. Good results were obtained by employing the exercises during work breaks for a period of four and a half months.

Raising Life Expectancy

Statistics from 1935 showed that the average life expectancy for farmers in China was 34.8 years. Beginning in 1949, as the material life and work conditions improved, the average life expectancy for the entire population greatly increased. In 1978, life expectancy in counties was 66.7 for males, 69.2 for females, and 67.9 overall. In big cities like Shanghai, Beijing, Tianjin, and Guangzhou, life expectancy reached 69.4 for males, 73.2 for females, and 71.3 overall. According to the 1982 National Census, there were over 77,830,000 persons above 60 years of age. Of these, females made up 53.5 percent and males 46.5 percent. Of 3,765 centenarians, 2,657 were females and 1,108 males, the oldest being 130 years old. The average life expectancy at birth in 1985 was 65.5 for males and 69.4 for females.

Sporting events, such as this annual Around the City Race in Beijing, are designed to provide competition for elite runners and encourage the general population to participate in regular exercise.

Establishing Enriching Spiritual and Cultural Life

The current rise of people's material life in China will create new demands on spiritual life. Sports and recreation will play an important role in meeting these demands. It is assumed that people will experience an enrichment in cultural life, increased interest in living, and enhanced vitality if people take part in physical training during their spare time or watch sports competitions and exhibitions. School sports programs will increase the feeling of school spirit. In rural areas, sports and recreation programs can aid modernization by helping to change old habits, customs, and superstitions.

Raising the Level of Performance in Athletic Competition

Developing sports in factories, mines, commercial enterprises, institutions, government organizations, and the countryside will undoubtedly lead to the emergence of great numbers of sports participants and qualified sportsmen, leading to an increase in the quality of sports skills and techniques at all levels of competition.

Government-Controlled Exercise

Various forms of group exercise are organized by governmental and industrial authorities or are encouraged by provision of time, space, or leadership.

Setting-Up Exercises to Radio Music—"Radio Calisthenics"

These are free-standing calisthenic exercises done under the guidance of music broadcast by radio stations. These exercises are simple and easy to perform, suited to people of different ages, sexes, and health conditions, and may be performed either by individuals or by groups of hundreds or thousands of people. In other words, they comprise a sports activity catering to the masses.

Setting-up exercises to radio music are divided into eight to ten sections of movements involving training of the upper limbs, lower limbs, and the trunk. The movements consist of flexing and extending, raising and flapping the arms, turning, balancing, and jumping.

Radio calisthenics began in 1951, when the All-China Sports Federation and the Central Broadcasting Administration Bureau announced that the Central People's Broadcasting Station and local broadcasting stations throughout the country would begin broadcasting programs of appropriate music. On November 24 of the same year, the broadcast of the first set of such exercises for adults occurred. From that time on, the broadcast of setting-up exercises to radio music has been carried out on a regular basis and has included the participation of personnel from many governmental offices, factories, and other large groups. For more than 30 years the State Physical Education and Sports Commission has promulgated 16 sets of setting-up exercises, of which 6 are for adults and 10 for juveniles and children.

Classes broadcast over the radio with music ("radio calisthenics") encourage many to participate in regular physical exercise.

Oil refinery workers take an exercise break.

Work-Break Exercises

In a proclamation issued in 1954, the government stated that, in order to improve the physiques and raise the working efficiency of staff members, two 10-minute breaks, one in the morning and the other in the afternoon, were to be offered for the purpose of performing work-break exercises in governmental organizations.

Production Exercises

Production exercises are industry-specific free-standing exercises designed to improve workers' stamina and productivity. Among them are the steel workers' exercise, the textile workers' exercise, the electronic industry workers' exercise, the building workers' exercise, the drivers' exercise, the coal miners' exercise, and the salesmen's exercise. The design of each of these exercises is based on the different types of work activities in which the workers are engaged. All these exercise routines move from simplicity to complexity in practice, from low load to high load in intensity, and from slowness to rapidity in speed and rhythm. Production exercises can usually be done to light music to enhance rhythmic sense and arouse the interest of the worker.

Individual Popular Sports

In addition to government-directed exercise, the Chinese enjoy participating in individual sports. Among the favorite activities are walking, jogging, and river swimming.

Walking and Jogging

Walking and jogging come under the category of aerobic exercises. The intensity of the activity involved is relatively low compared to many sports events and exercises. The activities can be employed for improving general physical condition, controlling and curing illness attributable to sedentary living, and preventing decline in health and bodily function for both the elderly and the middle aged. Additionally, these activities constitute an important measure for preventing and treating such chronic conditions as hypertension, coronary heart disease, diabetus mellitus, and obesity. Easy to perform and requiring no special facilities, these activities gain popularity with each passing day.

River Swimming

The Changjiang (Yangtze) River has been from time immemorial a natural barrier difficult to cross. At Wuhan, the River is 1,000 meters wide, with many torrents running at a velocity of 1.5-2.0 miles per second or faster.

Mao Zedong swam across the Changjiang at this location 13 times. The last time he did so was in 1966, when he was 73 years old. His practice lent a tremendous impetus to the sport of swimming across rivers, lakes, and bays. Beginning in 1956, in cities like Nanjing, Zhongqin, Hangzhou, Guangzhou, Fuzhou, Changsha, Nanning, Xi'an, and Shanghai, countless Chinese have swum across rivers and bays. Some locations even list river swimming as a competitive event to be held once a year.

Grand Popular Sports Competitions

In addition to the various sport activities identified and described, a number of mass sport events play important roles in the total sporting scene in China.

Workers' Games

Two National Workers' Athletic Meets were held in Beijing, in 1955 and 1985. At the second Meet, nine events (track-and-field, soccer, volleyball, basketball, table tennis, wushu, swimming, weight lifting, and bicycling) were included. There were 4,600 participants from 29 provinces and 3 sports clubs (Locomotive, Silver Eagle, and Hydroelectric).

Young Mongolians participate in a camel race in Hohhut.

Farmers' Games

Early in the summer of 1988, all the provinces selected farmer sports delegates to participate in the First National Farmers' Games, which were held on October 9, 1988, in Beijing. There were over 3,000 participants, including coaches. Seven competitive events (track-and-field, basketball, soccer, shooting, bicycling, table tennis, and wrestling) and one demonstration event (wushu) were included. All the participants of the National Games were selected through provincial meets.

Traditional Games of Minority Nationalities

In 1953, 1982, and 1986, three national Traditional Games were held in Beijing, Huhehaote, and Wulumuqi. There were over 3,000 participants in the third Games. Six competitive events (horse racing, wrestling, swinging, crossbow, diaoyang [sheep snatching with riding horse], and archery) and 115 demonstration items, such as bamboo jumping, springboard, and polo, were presented.

Acrobats of the Korean national minority in Yuen Bian use a teeter board to send each other hurtling skyward.

Summary

The retired factory worker performing taijiquan, the schoolboy practicing wushu with a sword, the contestant paddling in a dragon-boat race, the worker exercising with calisthenics to radio music, and the farmer playing for his provincial soccer team all participate in Chinese sport—whether traditional or popular. The Chinese government encourages participation in these events and many others by providing facilities, time, and organizational personnel.

Photo on facing page: The annual Ten-Thousand-People Marathon in Shanghai
attracts both elite and recreational runners.

Chapter 7

Development of Competitive Sports

WU Zhongyuan

Success in competitive sport brings fame to athletes and teams at all levels—local, regional, national, and international. The decision to make sports competition an integral part of China's total program of physical education and sport and to encourage elite competitors to attain the highest levels of achievement has vaulted China into the highest levels of international competition.

Competitive Sports in China's Physical Culture

The meaning of physical culture has long been a disputed issue among members of international sports circles, especially sports theorists and scholars. Should or should not competitive physical culture (also called competitive sports) be included in the category of physical culture? Among Chinese sports circles, some feel that competitive sports should not be included in the general category of physical culture. This, however, is the opinion of but a few people. Most Chinese sports theorists feel that physical culture includes two aspects: *physical training*, which helps people keep fit; and *competitive sports*, which increase the quality of performance and identify the top athletes.

Rong Gaotang, one of the prestigious leaders in China's sports, Olympic silver medal winner, and vice-president of the All-China Sports Federation, wrote in a preface to *Physical Culture*, a volume of the first *China Encyclopaedia*:

> [Physical culture] is an important way for people to build up their physical strength, strengthen their physique, and prolong their life span; it is a component part of the entire education in coordination with the moral, intellectual, and aesthetic education; in the form of competition, it is the content of people's cultural life and a link to strengthen relations between people of various countries. Although the three aspects differ in their aims, functions, and targets, they are interrelated. The three all take body activities as their basic means, aim at an all-round development of physical strength and improvement of physique, possess the contents of education and teaching and learning, and have the elements of competition and raising skill.

This view has been widely accepted in Chinese sports circles. The name of the national agency responsible for sports, the State Physical Education and Sports Commission, reflects this unifying concept. Physical education and competition are seen as inseparable aspects of physical culture as a whole.

The state has laid down the following three tasks for the work of physical culture:

- Carry out extensive mass sports activities, build up the people's health, and raise the health level of the whole nation.
- Foster and train outstanding athletes, raise the level of sporting techniques, and scale the heights of world sports.
- Enrich the people's spare-time cultural life and build up socialist ideology and culture.

Competitive sports occupy an important place in these objectives and the development of China's physical culture since the founding of the People's Republic in 1949 has made competitive sports an inseparable part of China's physical culture.

Popularization of Sport

Popularization of sports and an increase in competitive quality go hand in hand. As sports become more popular and attract more participants, the level of competition rises, leading to more interest and participation, which in turn generates higher standards of excellence and competition. It is this cycle that has rapidly raised the level of China's competitive athletes in the years since the founding of the People's Republic.

In prerevolutionary China, physical culture was poorly developed, and very few people took part in sports activities. Competitions were few. Consequently, the people had poor physiques and China had neither high-level competitions nor outstanding athletes. As late as the 1940s, many national records held by China's leading male athletes were lower than corresponding world women's records. In the three Olympiads the Chinese participated in from 1932 to 1948, no Chinese entered the finals in any event.

After the founding of the People's Republic of China in 1949, however, the levels of sporting techniques in China took an upward turn with the development of mass sports activities, especially with the increasing participation of youth and teenagers in sports. From 1956 to 1959, several world record holders and world champions emerged in China. Weight lifter Chen Jingkai

Zheng Fengrong broke the women's world high jump record in 1957 by clearing 1.79 meters.

Members of the Chinese women's volleyball team receive their gold medals at the 1984 Olympics held in Los Angeles.

broke the world record in clean and jerk nine times in a row. The outstanding woman high jumper Zheng Fengrong established a world record in 1957. Table tennis player Rong Guotuan captured the men's singles title at the World Table Tennis Championships in 1959.

These outstanding athletes distinguished themselves in the mass sports activities popularized in schools, factories, army barracks, and rural areas. Their achievements in creating world records or winning world championships inspired many more young people to exercise and compete. After Rong Guotuan won the world championship, the number of people playing table tennis throughout the country multiplied from several million to tens of millions. Similar expansion occurred in other sports. After the Chinese National Women's Volleyball Team was victorious five times in a row at the world championships, world cup tournament, and the Olympic Games, millions of teenagers took up the sport. As a result, China has long remained dominant in table tennis and volleyball. This has not only further popularized the sports but also helped more distinguished athletes to develop, enabling China to lead the world in these sports.

Competition

Competition is the most prominent feature of sports and does much to promote popularization and raise standards. Competition fires athletes with a sense of winning honor for the country and a desire to do better. Tens of millions of people are inspired to engage in sports activities, benefitting their bodies and minds and enriching their cultural life.

Competitive sports receive two-thirds of the expenditures allocated by the national government for physical culture. China has recently emphasized Olympic events in these development efforts. However, competitive activities are held every year not only for these Olympic events but also for mass sports events. Competitions in radio calisthenics, for example, are held between workshops or classes within factories and schools. These events are judged according to the number of participants, the quality of movements, and the level of group performances. Similar competitions can be held for taijiquan, mass swimming activities, and mountaineering.

The development of physical culture would be unimaginable without competitive activities. Competition is regarded as the pillar of competitive sports.

Spectating

As in other countries, the people who watch sports competitions outnumber those actually engaged in physical exercises. Spectating has been given a big boost by television, which is now broadcast to virtually all of China's urban and rural areas, making sports competitions available to tens of millions of sports fans.

Live television coverage of key matches or events in the Olympic Games, Asian Games, World Cup soccer tournament, World Volleyball Tournament, or World Table Tennis Championships, for instance, often attract hundreds of millions of viewers. During the World Cup Soccer Tournament held in Mexico, some of the matches were telecast live during early hours of the morning in China. Nevertheless, the number of viewers surpassed 100 million. Not long ago, world-class billiards players competed in China, drawing a TV audience of more than 100 million. According to statistics published by China's communication departments, traffic is lightest and buses carry the fewest passengers during live television coverage of major international sports competitions.

Sports competition is a means to educate the people in the spirit of patriotism. Every victory won by the Chinese women's volleyball team (which captured five world titles in a row) and by the Chinese table tennis players (who have dominated the sport for more than 20 years) has greatly inspired the people of the whole country. When Chinese athletes took 15 gold medals at the 23rd Olympic Games, it gave the one billion Chinese people an honor of epoch-making significance and made Chinese the world over feel proud. It is no exaggeration when people say that "one ball affects the hearts of hundreds of millions of people."

International Exchange

As a means of friendly exchange, sports competition strengthens both national harmony and international unity, aids in diplomacy, and promotes world peace and friendship. These benefits are gained both through large-scale international tournaments and in sports exchanges between countries. This is a major reason that various countries attach increasing importance to the Olympic Games and other international sports tournaments.

Exchanges not only raise the level of both countries' sporting techniques and promote the development of physical culture, but also enhance mutual understanding. Perhaps the most famous exchange took place in the early 1970s, when China invited the U.S. Table Tennis Team for a visit. This "ping pong diplomacy," as it was called, opened the door of relations between the two countries that had been shut for more than two decades.

Sports exchanges between China and other countries promote international friendship.

Training Athletes

In competitive sports, the key to developing talent and achieving good results is proper training. Only with organization in the training system, qualified coaches at all levels, as well as adequate facilities and scientific training methods can promising youngsters be developed into elite athletes who distinguish themselves in athletic contests both at home and abroad.

According to statistics, China had by 1985 fostered 102 male and 93 female world champions and 254 world record holders, 81 being females (see Tables 7.1 and 7.2).

Table 7.1 World Championships Won by Chinese Athletes (1959-1985)

Events	Number of events		Number of athletes	
	Total	Women's	Total	Women
Track-and-field	2	2	4	4
Diving	7	4	10	5
Weight lifting	10	0	6	0
Gymnastics	9	1	8	1
Shooting	7	5	11	9
Fencing	1	1	1	1
Windsurfing	2	2	2	2
Speed skating	1	0	1	0
Volleyball	1	1	22	22
Table tennis	7	4	46	21
Badminton	6	3	24	13
Acrobatic gymnastics	16	7	30	12
Go chess	1	0	6	0
Radio-controlled model ship competition	10	0	10	0
Parachuting	3	2	7	3
Radio-controlled airplane flying	4	0	7	0
Total	87	32	195	93

Table 7.2 World Records Broken or Established by Chinese Athletes (1956-1985)

Events	Number of events		Number of athletes	
	Total	Women's	Total	Women
Track-and-field	4	3	5	3
Swimming	1	0	3	0
Weight lifting	12	0	12	0
Shooting	28	13	53	28
Archery	13	11	13	12
Speed skating	1	0	2	0
Skin diving	1	0	1	0
Radio-controlled model ship competition	9	0	23	0
Motorboat racing	1	0	2	0
Parachuting	25	13	79	37
Radio-controlled model airplane flying	24	0	61	1
Total	119	40	254	81

Compared with advanced sports powers such as the United States, the Soviet Union, and the German Democratic Republic, these numbers cannot be considered great. However, that a country starting from scratch could reach such a level in a period of only 30 years is remarkable. A Chinese saying holds that "It takes ten years to grow trees, but a hundred years to rear people." The cultivation of exceptional athletes, like that of other kinds of talented people, is far more difficult than the mere construction of sports facilities.

How does China cultivate her outstanding athletes? This question is often raised by friends concerned with the development of China's sports. Here is a brief introduction.

Sports training in China is divided into three levels—primary, middle, and high—which are joined with each other to form a training system.

Primary-Level Training

Sports teams of the grass roots units, such as schools, factories, villages, enterprises, and government departments. These teams have a certain form of organization, train during the participants' spare time, and hold regular competitive events. The total number of such teams is tremendous. The sports teams of the primary and middle schools in particular are the bases from which China's outstanding athletes are drawn.

Special grass roots training programs. A school, factory, or a gymnasium or stadium can set up courses emphasizing one or two events to provide technical guidance to promising, interested teenagers.

Schools with a tradition of having excellent athletes in certain events. These are primary and middle schools that have traditionally stressed the development of particular sports and become recognized as leaders in them. The various government physical cultural agencies often provide limited funds to these schools and send experienced coaches to give technical guidance. Such schools have trained 25,000 outstanding athletes since 1980. Some of the athletes were subsequently sent to middle-level training schools; some were selected to sports teams of provinces, autonomous regions, municipalities, or army units; and some were admitted to physical culture institutions after passing entrance examinations.

For example, Julu Lu No. 1 Primary School of Shanghai has a tradition of developing table tennis. Ninety-five percent of the school's pupils take part in this sport. Honors won by players from this school have included the city championship, the national championship, and the team title at world championships.

Ordinary children's amateur sports schools. The first amateur sports school was founded in 1955. By 1957, 159 amateur sports schools had been established with an enrollment of 17,000 students. These schools were located in

92 cities and 20 counties in 23 provinces, autonomous regions, and munici-palities. China's athletic stars of the 1950s and 1960s, such as the world woman high-jump record breaker Zheng Fengrong and the world table tennis champion Zhuang Zedong, underwent training in amateur sports schools. It was stipu-lated in 1973 that amateur sports schools could only enroll children under the age of 17.

By 1985, the number of children's amateur sports schools throughout the country totalled 2,497, with 198,520 students and 10,609 full-time coaches. The students of the children's amateur sports schools are distributed among the ordinary primary and middle schools. They train 3 to 5 times a week, each session lasting 2 to 3 hours. After training for 3 to 5 years, the best one-quarter to one-third of these promising students are admitted to the middle level spare-time training programs (described in the next section). The remainder of the students no longer receive training but usually remain quite active in sports.

Middle-Level Training

Major amateur sports schools.   In 1959, Shanghai established major amateur sports schools designed to train the more promising graduates of the city's ordinary amateur sports schools. The students who live at these schools receive concentrated lessons and training, receiving a half-day of study and a half-day of training every day. This system does not affect the students' regular academic career but does enable them to undergo several years of systematic training under excellent conditions and instruction. By 1965, the country had 13 major amateur sports schools. Twenty years later, the number of these schools across the country reached 254, with 32,425 students and 3,069 full-time coaches.

Secondary sports schools.   These joint efforts of China's Physical Culture and Education departments are similar to the major amateur sports schools. The teachers for academic classes are provided by the educational depart-ment and their salaries and teaching facilities are paid from educational funds. Coaches are provided by the physical culture department while their salaries and all sportswear, sports equipment, and facilities are paid from physical culture funds.

The secondary sports school has the same curriculum as the ordinary second-ary school except that it is more advanced in spare-time sports training. In the course of their 3 to 6 years' study (3 years each for junior and senior middle schooling), the students, according to their levels and achievements, can be admitted to the teams of a province, an autonomous region, a munici-pality, or even to the national teams. The age of 15 is the youngest at which students may be sent to the teams of women's basketball, women's volley-ball, women's track-and-field, table tennis, badminton, tennis, and speed skating, while 17 is the youngest age for the teams of men's basketball, men's volleyball, men's track-and-field, soccer, weight lifting, cycling, fencing, baseball, softball, team handball, ice hockey, water polo, wrestling, and rowing. Students not admitted to the teams may continue their study after passing entrance examinations from junior to senior middle schools and from senior middle schools to institutions of higher learning. By 1985, the country had 87 secondary sports schools, with 10,264 students and 950 full-time coaches.

Physical culture and sports schools.   These 4-year vocational secondary schools cultivate the future athletes of China. Those graduating students who are not sent to the teams of a province, an autonomous region, or a municipality generally become physical culture teachers at primary or secondary schools. By 1983, the country had 27 physical culture and sports schools, with 5,710 students and nearly 1,000 full-time coaches.

Statistics in 1985 showed that the number of students specializing in a certain event and undergoing regular and systematic training throughout the country totalled 87,000. Most of them were between the ages of 7 and 17. Most of the students were engaged in track-and-field, swimming, gymnastics, soccer, basketball, volleyball, table tennis, or shooting—more than 10,000 in track-and-field, more than 5,000 in basketball, and between 2,000 and 3,000 in each of the other events. From these students, China's athletic elite are expected to arise in the 1990s and early in the next century.

High-Level Training

About one-quarter of the students who go through middle-level training continue to the next stage, high-level training. High-level training takes several forms, as follows:

Sports teams organized by and representing provinces, autonomous regions, and municipalities.   These teams compete in 10 to 40 events, depending on the area's development and other conditions. The number of athletes on each team ranges from 200 to over 1,000. For example, the city of Shanghai, which is more advanced than other cities, has a team of more than 1,000 athletes engaged in 38 events. Qinghai province, a remote area that is less developed in sports, has a team of 255 engaged in 15 events. All these athletes have distinguished themselves in their own localities. Most teams also serve as physical culture technical institutes similar to institutions of higher learning. Their primary task is to cultivate top-notch athletes and coaches.

Sports teams organized in the army and the trades.   The People's Liberation Army attaches great importance to developing physical culture and has established sports teams at various levels. A team representing the whole army competes in nearly 30 events. The army team is known as the "August First" team, commemorating the founding anniversary of the Chinese People's

Liberation Army. The team makes strict demands on athletes and is highly disciplined. In many events, the army team fields first-rate athletes in both domestic and international contests. Five players from the army women's volleyball team have played on the Chinese national squad. Many army basketball players have played for the national team, which is the Asian men's basketball champion. China's sole woman gymnastics world champion on the uneven bars, Ma Yanhong, also came from the army. Among the athletes in the army team, some were trained by the army itself and some were recruited from major amateur sports schools, secondary sports schools, and other schools. In addition to the sports teams in the army system, there are also high-level sports teams from trade organizations such as the railways, coal mining, and water conservancy and power ministries. Excellent coaches are frequently invited to help in training.

Physical culture institutes and institutions of higher learning.   The physical culture institute is a sports institution of higher learning. It fosters not only teachers of physical culture but also coaches, scientific research personnel, governmental officials of physical culture, and outstanding athletes. The

The Navy of the People's Republic of China encourages sports activities among its sailors.

14 physical culture institutes in the country have their own sports teams, the members of which are required to fulfill not only their school lessons but also their tasks for training. The competitive sports school set up by Beijing Physical Culture Institute enrolls promising children from the ordinary and major children's amateur sports schools and from other channels. Most of this school's graduates are admitted to the sports teams of the provinces, autonomous regions, municipalities, the Chinese People's Liberation Army, or the industrial systems. Some are admitted directly to the national teams.

The national team represents the highest stage in top-level training. Members of the national teams are selected from the teams of the provinces, autonomous regions, municipalities, the Chinese People's Liberation Army, and other systems through assessment in national competition and other evaluation. The State Physical Education and Sports Commission has a bureau in charge of the training of the national teams. Training bases for the national teams have been established in Beijing, Qinhuangdao in Hebei province, Kunming in Yunnan province, and Zhangzhou in Fujian province.

The total number of athletes engaged in systematic high-level training throughout the country is less than 20,000.

The three-level training system has proved successful in fostering outstanding athletes and raising the technical skills of sports. It was organized by using the experience of other countries for reference while taking into consideration China's unique conditions. Of course, there are still areas that call for improvement. China still has a long way to go to become a top-ranked sports power in the world. In the fifty-odd sports events practiced in the country, the total number of athletes undergoing regular and systematic training is less than 250,000, far less than in the United States or the Soviet Union. Therefore, there are often temporary shortages of athletes in some events. Another problem is that the scientific level of training is not high, especially in some basic events like track-and-field and swimming. The level of China's sports training facilities is also comparatively low.

Chinese sports circles are exerting fresh efforts in the hope of gaining new breakthroughs in the 21st century.

Types of Competitions and Sports Personnel

In a sport program as comprehensive as China's, competitive events are organized in a skill level tier system. The various events must be organized and officiated by persons who are well prepared and highly competent.

Classification of Competitions

China practices a unified competition system and a national competition program. A concerted effort is made to have major domestic tournaments be followed by major international ones and grass roots competitions be followed by regional and national events. China's sports competitions take the following forms:

Comprehensive national sports meets.   The largest in scale is the Games of the People's Republic of China or "national games" for short. These games are characterized by a large number of events and many participants. The first national games were held in Beijing in 1959. Thirty-six competitive events and six exhibition events were held. More than 10,000 athletes represented 29 provinces, autonomous regions, and municipalities, as well as the Chinese People's Liberation Army. The second national games were held in 1965. It was originally planned that the national games would be held every four years, but they were suspended due to the Cultural Revolution (1966-1976); it was not until 1975 that the third national games were held. The fourth and fifth national games were held in 1979 and 1983, respectively. Beijing was the venue for the first four games and, starting with the fifth games, various provinces, autonomous regions, and municipalities could apply to host them. The fifth national games were hosted by Shanghai, the sixth in Guangzhou, and the seventh games will be held in the city of Chengdu. The first four national games included winter sports, which were held separately from the summer games in terms of time and venue. Beginning with the fifth, the national games were divided into the national games and the national winter games. The national games are the biggest sports festivals of the country. They play an important role in promoting the development of the country's physical culture.

The national juvenile games.   These games were first conducted in 1986. Participating teams and events are generally the same as the national games. Different age groups of athletes are established for different events. Track-and-field events are divided into group A (boys: 18 and 19; girls: 17 and 18) and group B (boys: under 17; girls: under 16); swimming into group A (15-17) and group B (under 14). Shooting has an age limit of 20; archery, fencing, wrestling, and judo of 18; boys' gymnastics of 15; and girls' gymnastics of 13. The juvenile games are held every 4 years for the purpose of fostering and selecting athletes for the Olympic Games.

National competitions held in the worker, army, and school systems. There are national workers' games, army games, national university games, and national middle school games. The time, events, and rules of competition are decided upon by the agencies or groups concerned.

National championships for particular sports.   This kind of championship is held every year for various events. A participating team may represent a province, autonomous region, municipality, branch of the military, or an industrial system. In certain sports, some regions of China will not have an athlete or team to represent them, and competing teams for national championships may come from only a handful of cities or smaller geopolitical entities.

This uneven representation occurs in winter sports such as ice hockey and skating, in the water sports of rowing and yachting, and in tennis. Factors such as regional weather conditions, local access to appropriate bodies of water, and area acceptance of a certain sport influence which regions produce which athletes. A steamy inland village that shows no interest in skating will not produce many ice hockey players.

National competitions of different classifications.   The purpose of these competitions is to give the athletes (and their teams) an opportunity to compete against athletes of similar skill levels. National league A and league B matches (as based on competancy level) are held for soccer, basketball, and volleyball, with a system of promotion and demotion between leagues. The matches are held in two stages—the first stage in the first half of the year and the second stage in the latter half. Competitions are also held for athletes of different classes in track-and-field, gymnastics, and swimming. Two or three competitions are held for individual events every year.

China's National Soccer League A offers the highest level of competition for this sport.

Duel meets.   These contests are held among athletes (or teams) drawn from different regions (such as East China or Northeast China) or systems (such as different industrial systems or schools).

Competitions through communication.   These competitions can be held for those events whose results are determined by such objective criteria such as time, distance, or weight. Participants can hold contests within their own units according to standardized rules of competition, then tabulate the results and send them to a coordinating sponsor who determines the standings.

Invitational tournaments.   A region, a city, or other unit can hold this kind of tournament, in which athletes or teams of the same level from other areas are invited to participate.

There are many other athletic competitions. In the past, competitive activities were usually sponsored by sports departments or industrial systems. In recent years, socialized sports have increasingly drawn the interests of big factories, mines, enterprises, collectives, and even individual industrialists and businesspeople in sponsoring regional and even national sports competitions. It is interesting to note that a peasant in Shangdong province founded a national farmers' games.

Skill Classifications for Sport Personnel

By rating quality of performance and competition, classification systems provide athletes, coaches, and referees with recognition of attainment as well as proper matching of ability level.

Skill classification system for athletes.   The State Physical Education and Sports Commission formulated and put into practice a system designed to encourage athletes to improve their skills. Under the system, athletes are arranged into six skill classes—international master of sports, master of sports, and sportsman first class, second class, third class, and junior class. An athlete qualified in any of the six classes will be conferred the corresponding title, given a certificate and badge, and entitled to participate in contests of that class. The technical standards of various classes are established with regard to the technical levels and conditions of all Chinese athletes and in reference to the standards of international competition. An international master of sports is usually competing at international standards. Table 7.3 shows the standards for some events of track-and-field.

According to statistics from 1985, the athletes who qualified according to the standards of various skill classes numbered more than 67,000, among which 59 men and 54 women were international masters of sports and 550 men and 302 women were masters of sports.

Skill classification system for coaches.   Coaches are arranged in the following classes: head coach, coach, and assistant coach. They coach for national teams, provincial teams, and in spare-time sports schools. There are about 30,000 professional coaches in China.

Skill classification system for referees.   According to this system, referees are arranged in five classes: international referee, national referee, and referee first class, second class, and third class. The number of classified referees in China exceeds 60,000; nearly 100 of them are international referees and more than 400 are national referees.

**Table 7.3   Chinese Skill Classification Standards
for Some Track-and-Field Events (1987)**

Events	Classification					
	National master of sports	Master of sports	First-class athlete	Second-class athlete	Third-class athlete	Junior-class athlete
100-m sprints						
Male	10.30 sec	10.64 sec	10.94 sec	11.74 sec	12.64 sec	13.24 sec
Female	11.41 sec	11.94 sec	12.34 sec	13.04 sec	14.04 sec	14.84 sec
High jump						
Male	2.27 m	2.12 m	2.00 m	1.83 m	1.60 m	1.50 m
Female	1.90 m	1.80 m	1.75 m	1.56 m	1.40 m	1.30 m
Discus						
Male	63.00 m (2 kg)	54 m	49.50 m	38 m	29 m	28 m (1.5 kg)
Female	62.98 m (1 kg)	55 m	51 m	39 m	31 m	25 m

Examination and Approval of National Sports Records

All major formal competitions are refereed by qualified national referees. An athlete who breaks a national record at such a competition may apply for recognition of the record as a new national record. It may then be approved and recognized by the relevant sports association. Such national records are compiled and released in January of the following year by the state.

Summary

A comprehensive system of competitive sports for a nation with a population exceeding one billion people requires tremendous organization and many skilled and dedicated administrators, coaches, and referees. With goals of both mass participation and promotion of Chinese athletes among the world's elite, elaborate measures have been undertaken to encourage the fullest possible development of competitive sports in China.

Photo on facing page: Ma Yanhong won the gold medal in the uneven parallel bars at the 23rd Olympiad in Los Angeles.

Chapter 8

Outstanding Athletes and Their Coaches

LU Xianwu
LIN Shuying

Because of China's long isolation from the rest of modern civilization and its resultant lack of involvement in world sport competition, China was not considered to be part of the international sporting scene until the second half of the 20th century. However, as a result of national attention to improving the fitness of all Chinese and helping top athletes attain their full potential, China emerged rapidly into the circle of champions for a number of sports events.

Winners of International Competitions

In 1936, a German newspaper carried a cartoon depicting several Chinese searching for Olympic medals beside a large goose egg (symbolizing a zero). It was a satire on the semifeudal and semicolonial China and an insult to the Chinese people as well. But it was not entirely groundless. Before 1949, China had taken part in the Olympic games three times, represented on each occasion by a single pole vaulter, Fu Baolu, who gained access to the finals.

Now, such a time is gone forever. In 1984, the sharpshooter Xu Haifeng captured the first gold medal ever for China at the Los Angeles Olympics, ushering in a new era in China's sports. Watching the national flag of the People's Republic of China being hoisted for the first time at the Olympic games, a 70-year-old overseas Chinese, Wang Minxin, was moved to tears, exclaiming, ''We've got a gold medal at last! We are no longer the sick men of East Asia!''

Since the People's Republic of China was founded in 1949, China has produced 231 world champions and broken 302 world records. During the 8 years (1979-1986) following the Third Plenary Session of the 11th Congress of the Chinese Communist Party Central Committee, China won 201 world championships, accounting for 87 percent of the total won since the founding of New China, and broke or exceeded 125 world records, representing 41% of the respective total. In both the 1982 and 1986 Asian Sports Games, China took the lead in gold medals. At the 23rd Olympics held in Los Angeles

Xu Haifeng was the first Chinese to win an Olympic gold medal (Los Angeles, 1984).

in 1984, China surprised the world by capturing 15 gold medals (ranking fourth in this respect among the 140 participating countries and regions), 8 silver medals, and 9 bronze medals. At the 24th Summer Olympic Games, the overall results were respectable but rather disappointing. While Chinese competitors in women's swimming and diving, men's diving, and men's weight lifting produced highly impressive results, expected medals in other sport events such as gymnastics and women's volleyball did not materialize. Chinese athletes brought home 5 gold, 11 silver, and 12 bronze medals from Seoul.

China has emerged as a sports giant of Asia and is now becoming a world sports power.

Table Tennis

China's first world champion was Rong Guotuan, a table tennis player from the Zhongshan County of Guangdong province. At the 25th World Table Tennis Championships held in 1959 in Dortmund, Federal Republic of Germany, Rong Guotuan won the men's singles championship. Rong's victory smashed the myth that world championships were unattainable by the Chinese and ushered in a new era in Chinese table tennis, one that has lasted for 30 years. In the 26th World Championships held in Beijing in 1961, Chinese players captured the men's team title as well as the championships in men's and women's singles.

During the 10 years of the chaotic Cultural Revolution (1966-1976), Chinese table tennis suffered a great deal. In 1971, however, Chinese players returned to the arena of the World Championships. At the 36th World Championships held in Yugoslavia in 1981, Chinese players surprised the world by taking

Rong Guotuan was China's first table tennis world champion.

all seven titles, a new record in the 55-year history of the world Table Tennis championships.

In the period from 1959 to 1987, Chinese table tennis players won 53.5 championships, 40 second place finishes, and 74 third place finishes at the World Championships. They also won 23 championships, 13 second places, and 6 third places at 4 Asian sports games between 1974 and 1986; and 39 championships, 32 second places, and 40 third places at 8 Asian table tennis championships between 1972 and 1986. China also produced a large number of top-notch players, represented by Rong Guotuan, Xu Yinsheng, Li Furong, Zhang Xieling, Ling Huiqin, Zheng Mingzhi, Zhang Li, Guo Yaohua, Cao Yahua, and Jiang Jialiang. They won the world championship in various divisions over one hundred times, establishing an unprecedented record.

Women's Volleyball

In the 1980s, the Chinese women's volleyball team emerged from mediocrity and won five world championships in succession from 1981 to 1986, becoming the world's first winner of five successive championships. This did not happen by chance. Outstanding players such as Sun Jinfang, Cao Huiying, Lang Ping, Zhang Rongfang, Liang Yan, and Yang Xilan were nurtured by the painstaking efforts of several generations of volleyball coaches and players. At Seoul in 1988, the team finished with the favorites, but failed to take a medal.

Gymnastics

Chinese men's and women's gymnastics teams took their places among the world's six top nations in this sport in the 1960s. It is only during the last 7 to 8 years, however, that China has become one of the world's gymnastic giants. In the 20th World Gymnastics Championships held in 1979, Ma Yahong became China's first world gymnastics champion. Two years later, China was runner-up in the women's team competition in the 21st World Gymnastic Championships. In 1983, the Chinese men's team composed of Li Ning, Tong Fei, Lou Yun, Li Yuejiu, Li Xiaoping, and Xu Zhiqiang won the world men's team title for the first time. In the 1984 Los Angeles Olympics, China's gymnasts won 5 gold medals, accounting for one-third of the total China took at the games. At the 1988 Seoul Olympics, Lau Yun in the men's vault won the only Chinese gymnastics medal. Altogether, Chinese gymnasts have won 23 gold medals at the Olympics, World Championships, and World Cup Competitions.

Li Ning, a member of China's 1983 world championship gymnastics team, was considered one of the world's best gymnasts.

Badminton

Highly skilled Chinese badminton players were once unfairly excluded from the world competitions before the restoration of their seat on the International Badminton Federation (IBF) in 1981. When the IBF and the World Badminton Federation merged in the early 1980s, China recovered its lawful right. Within only 6 years, outstanding Chinese players such as Yang Yang, Han Jian, Luan Jin, Zhang Ailing, Li Lingwei, Ling Ying, Wu Dixi, Xu Rong, and Wu Jianqiu won a total of 26 world championships. The Chinese men's and women's teams gained the world's highest trophies for badminton—the Thomas Cup and the Yeub Cub.

Diving

During the Period of Reform (since 1978), the Chinese diving team has won a total of 23 world championships. Among them are 6 team titles, one individual championship in platform diving at the 1984 Los Angeles Olympics, and 6 championships gained at the 1985 Fourth World Diving Cups. Chen Xiaoxia, Shi Meiqin, Li Hongping, Li Yihua, and Zhou Jihong have become world famous divers.

In the 24th Olympic Games (Seoul), China achieved spectacular success. For the women, Xu Yanmei won the gold in the platform while in the springboard, Gao Min and Li Qing of China took both gold and silver, respectively. For the men, Xiong Ni took the silver in platform while Tan Liangde took silver and Lin Deliang took bronze in the springboard. Altogether, China took 6 of the 12 medals.

Gao Min received a gold medal in the women's 3-meter dive at the 1988 Olympic Summer Games in Seoul.

Weightlifting

China's first world record was established by the bantamweight lifter, Chen Jingkai. This took place on June 7, 1956, in a Shanghai stadium during a competition between Chinese teams and a visiting Soviet team. Twenty-year-old Chen, an army athlete from Guangdong, set a new world record by successfully jerking 133 kg, exceeding the world record of 132.5 kg then held by Winch of the United States. Following Chen Jingkai, the athletes Huang Qianghui, Zhao Qingkui, Li Jiyuan, Ye Haobo, Chen Manling, Xiao Mingxiang, Ji Fayuan, Deng Guoyin, Chen Weiqiang, and Wu Shude created new world records in succession.

In 1979, Wu Shude gained the gold medal in the 52 kg class competition of the World Weight Lifting Championships, becoming China's first weight lifting champion. In 1984, China's weight lifters won four gold medals in the Los Angeles Olympics. In 1986, He Shuoqiang smashed the world record in the 52 kg class snatch to become China's 37th world record breaker.

In the 24th Olympic Games, China took 5 medals. He Yinqiang won the silver medal in the 56 kg class. Four bronze medals went to He Shuoqiang in the 52 kg class, Liu Shoubin in the 56 kg class, Ye Huanming in the 60 kg class, and Li Jinhe in the 67.5 kg class.

Chen Jingkai, Huang Qianghui, and Zhao Qingkui each set world records in weight lifting.

Track-and-Field

China's first world record holder in the high jump was Zheng Fengrong, a young woman from Shandong. In November 1957, Zheng cleared 1.77 meters, breaking the record of 1.76 meters held by McDaniel of the United States. The first woman world record holder of China, Zheng was praised as "the swallow heralding the spring of China's sports." Following her came many outstanding track-and-field athletes. In 1965, three Chinese athletes were ranked among the world elite. They were Chen Jianquan (men's 100-meter sprint, 10.0 sec); Ni Zhiqin (men's high jump, 2.25 meters) and Cui Ling (men's 110-meter hurdles, 13.5 sec). In 1970, Ni Zhiqin established the world high jump record of 2.29 meters. In a period of less than one year, between 1983 and 1984, high jumper Zhu Jianhua three times bettered the world record.

Beginning in 1983, China's women walkers Xu Yongjiu, Yan Hong, Guan Ping, Li Sujie, Jin Bingjie, and Yu Heping have broken world records or created the world's best results for the year 13 times and captured 4 world championships.

Shooting

Target and clay pigeon shooting in China enjoy broad appeal. Since the 1950s, hundreds of thousands of people have taken part in shooting exercises every year. In 1959, China found her first world-record-breaking marksman at the First National Sports Games. He was Zhang Hong. During the 1960s and 1970s, a group of excellent shooters including Dong Xiangyi consistently scored better results than the world records, though these scores went unrecognized because China was not a member of the International Shooting Union. From 1981 to 1983, after China regained its status in the federation, Wu Lanying, Feng Meimei, and Shao Weiping captured the team or singles titles in the women's two-way clay pigeon competitions in three successive World Championships and officially set world records in the event. At the world championships held in 1985 and 1986, the Chinese women's team retained its group title and won the women's team and singles titles of trap shooting. Li Xin exceeded the world women's prone shooting record in standard rifle, while the men's team won the title of moving target shooting. In the 1987 World Cup competitions, 18-year-old Li Cuihong won two gold medals in the women's moving target pistol competition. At the 1988 Olympic Games, Xu Haifeng took the bronze medal in men's air pistol and Huang Shiping took the silver in running game target for men.

Archery

China's archery team made its debut on the world scene in the early 1960s. It soon surpassed world group records 6 times, and Li Shulan alone exceeded world records in women's singles 11 times. Beginning in the 1980s, China formally took part in international standard archery competition. At the 1984 Olympics, Li Lingjuan won the all-round championship for women's singles in the double archery event and smashed five world records. At the 34th World Archery Championships held in 1987, Ma Xiangjun seized the women's individual title.

Other Sports

In the field of go (weiqi) and chess games, Chinese players have displayed excellent talents. Outstanding go players, including Chen Zude and Nie

Weiping, have dominated the international go world for many years. Liu Shilan, a woman chess player from Sichuan, was China's first winner of the international supermaster title as well as the first Asian to enter the world's top eight.

China's woman fencer, Luan Jujie, captured the gold medal of women's epee contest at the 1984 Los Angeles Olympics, becoming the first Olympic fencing champion from the Orient in 60 years. Gao Fenglian from Inner Mongolia became China's first world judo champion in 1986.

In mountain climbing, China's Wang Fuzhou, Qu Yinhua, and Tibetan mountaineers Gong Bu and Pan Duo were the first to climb Mount Qomolangma (Mt. Everest), the world's highest peak, from the north side. They are regarded as heros by all Chinese and around the world.

In 1960, Chinese mountaineers were the first to climb Qomolangma (Mt. Everest), the world's highest mountain, from the north side.

In model ship navigation, parachute-jumping, and model aviation, Chinese athletes broke world records 30, 40, and 60 times, respectively. In the latter two events, China also won two world championships.

Chinese acrobats have won many world championships for their motherland. The women's basketball and handball teams have ranked among the world's top three. The women's softball team took the second place in the first world championship tournament it ever took part in. Chinese swimmers have created world records. The Chinese windsurfing team has repeatedly won titles in regional and worldwide competitions. Chinese women bridge players have been honored with the title of world's supermaster. In 1963,

Luo Zhihuan and Wang Jinyu broke the world record in men's all-round speed skating. Twenty-four years later, in the Sixth World Winter Games, 18-year-old Li Jinyan smashed the women's world record for 3,000 meters indoor speed skating.

Chinese athletes have approached or reached world-class levels in 25 of the 60 single events included in track-and-field, weight lifting, and speed skating. With the current effort at modernization, China's sports are progressing rapidly.

Factors Behind China's Sport Success

People may wonder how so many Chinese athletes have mounted the awards platforms lately. What are the specific reasons for the emergence of so many world champions and record breakers?

China Takes Advantage of Its Vast Territory and Rich Athletic Resources

China has a population of over one billion, with a vast territory covering several climatic zones. This provides a wide variety of talent for all kinds of sports events. To cultivate this talent, Chinese government agencies at all levels attach great importance to physical culture and mass sports activities from which elite athletes can arise.

China's outstanding athletes come for the most part from urban areas. Zhang Xieling, a table tennis player who won fame for his soft but changeable chopping technique back in the 1960s, was a worker at the Shanghai Steam Turbine Factory. Many prominent athletes come directly from schools. Lang Ping, the superstar of women's volleyball, used to be a student in Beijing Chaoyang Middle School. When she entered the school in 1974, 13-year-old Lang Ping soon became very active in sports. Her physical culture teacher, Meng Jinhua, a member of the Southwest China Volleyball Team in the 1950s, was seeking members for the school's volleyball team. She spotted the 1.72 meter tall, slim, and weak Lang Ping at once. Lang left her basketball partners and became a volleyball player. Through track-and-field exercises, Lang improved her physical strength and flexibility. She worked hard and became the team's main attacker. Later, Lang enrolled at Beijing No. 2 Spare-Time Sports School and began to receive regular physical training. In the early 1980s, Lang Ping finally became one of the world's best attackers. Her teammate Sun Jinfang, the famous setter, is also from a sports school. Other sports-school graduates include Li Ning, nicknamed the "prince of gymnastics," Chen Xiaoxia, the "empress of diving," Wu Shude, the "Oriental Samson," and the outstanding table tennis player Xie Saike.

The vast rural areas have also nurtured many athletes, especially during the last few years, due to a stable political situation and a rapidly growing rural economy. For instance, Wang Xiuting, the gold medalist in the 10,000-meter run at the 10th Asian Sports Games, used to be a country girl in a village of Laoshan County, Shandong province. Gao Fenglian, world champion of the over-72-kilogram-class judo, was originally a farmer in Inner Mongolia. As a child, she began to help her parents with field work. At the age of 16, she was already 1.80 meters in height and 75 kilograms in weight. She became so strong that she could do as much work as two strong young men could. Gao's road to the sports field was not smooth, however. She was twice rejected by the prefectural spare-time sports school for basketball and track-and-field training. Finally, a judo coach recognized her potential talents, and in 1980 Gao began her judo training. Three years later she participated in the world championships for the first time and won third-place in the judo competition. Now, measuring 1.86 meters tall and weighing 114 kilograms, Gao has become a rising star on the judo stage.

The People's Liberation Army (PLA) constitutes a major school for training athletes. Three of the ten best track-and-field athletes in 1986 came from the PLA. Twenty-eight of the 94 gold medals China gained at the 10th Asian Sports Games were contributed by athletes from the PLA. Cao Huiying, Yang Xi, Chen Zhaodi, Yang Xilan, and Li Yanjun are prominent women volleyball players from the PLA who, with their teammates, won five world championships in succession.

China is a multinational country. Minority nationality athletes have contributed significantly to the development of China's sports. Among the outstanding are Gong Bu and Pan Duo, two Tibetan women mountaineers who have conquered Mount Qomolongma (Mt. Everest); Mu Xiangsong, a world-record-breaking swimmer of the Hui nationality; Jin Dongxiang, a Manchu nationality girl who has smashed the world's shooting record; Luo Zhihuan, a 1,500-meter world speed-skating champion of Korean nationality; and gymnasts Li Ning and Huang Qun of the Zhuang nationality.

China Has Successfully Established a Three-Level Training System

As discussed in the previous chapter, a three-level (primary, intermediate, and high level) training system guarantees the production of large numbers of outstanding athletes, coaches, and sports management personnel. This is an important element in promoting physical culture and raising the level of sports competition in China.

People usually compare the three-level training system to a pyramid. According to incomplete statistics gathered by the State Physical Education and Sports Commission from 20 provinces, autonomous regions, and municipalities during the period from 1980 to 1983, the country's grass roots physical training schools for conventional sports events (the base of the pyramid) produced 23,070 potential athletes. From this group, 15,715 entered key city (prefectural) and county (district) spare-time sports classes, full-time sports schools, and provincial sports schools. Another 1,270 were sent to the sports teams of provinces, autonomous regions, municipalities, and army units, and 2,312 were enrolled in sports colleges (Figure 8.1). Statistics from the state sports teams and provincial and municipal teams of Beijing, Shanghai, Liaoning, Henan, Shandong, Sichuan, Guangdon, Shaanxi, and Fujian show that 85% of their outstanding athletes came from spare-time sports schools. Approximately 80 percent of the gold medalists at the Ninth Asian Sports Games held in 1982 had received training in spare-time sports schools. More than 90% of the 24 athletes who won a total of 15 golds at the 1984 Los Angeles Olympics had been in amateur schools. These statistics show that the three-level training system has great vitality and can be compared to a factory turning out prominent athletes.

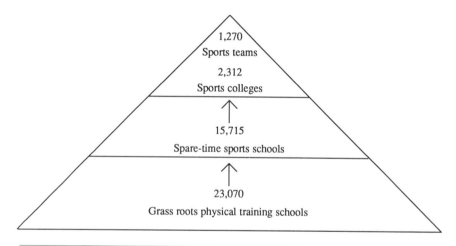

Figure 8.1 The number of athletes who advanced through China's three-level training system from 1980 to 1983.

The three-level system is not yet perfect and needs to be improved. In recent years, the three-level system has been developing in several ways. The development of intermediate-layer sports schools and single event training schools has been especially emphasized. At present, China has approximately 100 schools of this kind, two-and-a-half times as many as in 1984. At the same time, various types of physical training centers, sports clubs, as well as primary sports schools and kindergartens have been developed. All these have provided more opportunities for children and youth to receive training.

China Distributes Key Sports Events and Builds Intensive Training Centers

It has proven highly effective to concentrate China's limited financial and material resources for developing major Olympic sports events. In such a vast country, the quality of coaching, experience in training high-level athletes, and condition of training facilities vary greatly from place to place. Therefore, by assigning different key sports events to different administrative areas China makes the most of local advantages and initiative. For instance, the city of Dolian in Liaoning province has become a center for soccer, Nanning, Guangxi province, produces great divers, and cold, northern Harbin, in Heilongjiang has become a capital for skaters. Thus the state gives differing levels of support to different sports in the various regions of China. If the 1986 Asian Games are any indication, the system seems to be working. China ranked first in the number of gold medals at the games, and all 15 gold medals in shooting were won by athletes from the areas in which state support of shooting programs was concentrated. Most of the golds in weight lifting and track-and-field were also won by athletes from areas in which those sports received concentrated support.

A key feature of this system of concentrated support is the establishment of state-of-the-art training centers in the appropriate areas. Such a training center helped lead to the great success of the women's volleyball team. In addition, training centers can also help train coaches of junior spare-time sports schools.

China Emphasizes Competition

Competition, the most conspicuous characteristic of sports, is considered the best means of discovering and nurturing elite athletes. China began to establish its own sports competition system in the 1950s. The National Sports Meet and the National Youth Sports Meet are held once every 4 years, usually preceding the Asian and the Olympic Games. The National Municipal Sports Meet, the College Students Games, and various top-level single-event competitions are organized once or twice a year. There are also many other sports events such as regional competitions, competitions of junior and amateur athletes, traditional sports events, and sponsored and subsidized games. All these help in the discovery, selection, and training of talented athletes.

Of course, training conditions, environment, policies, and programs are but objective elements for athletes' success. If the athletes do not practice hard and tenaciously or fail to grasp the laws of scientific training, they will never be able to capture world championships.

In the men's singles final of the 39th World Table Tennis Tournament held in New Delhi in 1987, Chinese player Jiang Jialiang fell behind his Swedish opponent by a score of 16 to 20. Instead of giving up, Jiang went all out to catch up and finally win by a score of 24-22, capturing his second world championship. What accounts for Jiang's success? On one hand, he made full use of the advantages provided by China's system for athlete development. On the other, he brought his own initiative into full play. In 1970, Jiang's father, a table tennis fan, sent him to a spare-time sports school in Zhong Shan County, Guangdon province. Considering Jiang's physical condition, his first coach, Mr. Zheng, thought him to have great potential. Zheng taught him the traditional Chinese technique of playing—a pen-hold grip and fast attack over the table. At the age of nine, Jiang switched to the provincial sports school. There, coached by Zu Yan, he twice won the provincial championship for juniors under 12. At 13, he was named to the provincial team, where he was coached by Cai Mingshu, a former national player. He placed fifth in the men's singles during the Fourth National Sports Meet at the age of 15 and was then admitted to the national team. When he was 19, he took part in the 37th World Table Tennis Tournament, contributing a great deal to China's capture of the male team championship. Twice he won the world championship, in 1985 and 1987. His success resulted mainly from the training he received, including more than 7 years of intensive training with the national team, as well as from his hard work and tenacity. But his childhood dream also played a role. China's first world champion, Rong Guotuan, was from Jiang's hometown in Zhongshan County. When a child, Jiang was determined to be another Rong Guotuan. He has never forgotten the fact that his success was due in great part to the opportunities available to him in the Chinese system.

The Chinese Respect Successful Athletes

Prominent athletes are the devoted sons and daughters of the Chinese people. They dedicate their youth to winning glory for the people. Conversely, the Chinese people love and praise their athletes and coaches and respect all who make athletic contributions to the country. There are countless examples of this relationship.

Two hundred and four combat heroes stationed in the Faka Mountain, Guangxi province, sent two military medals to Xu Haifeng and Zeng Guoqiang when they won the first two Olympic gold medals for China in Los Angeles. They wrote in their letter: "The two military medals we are sending you are the crystallization of our blood and youth. May they shine together with the gold medals around your neck."

In 1981, after China's women's volleyball team won their first world championship, 30,000 congratulatory telegrams and letters poured in like snowflakes. In their Zhuzhou training center, Fujian province, stand their group statues. In Guanxi's Liuzhou, the native city of Li Ning, champion of the Olympics, World Gymnastics Tournament, and the World Cup, a 1.90 meter statue has recently been completed in his honor. A "Three-Hero-Cup Table Tennis Tournament" has been initiated to cherish the memory of Rong Guotuan, China's first table tennis world champion, his coach Fu Qifang, and his fellow player Jiang Yongning.

When athletes run into difficulties, people often generously offered their help and encouragement. In short, Chinese people and their athletes and coaches are one heart and one mind and share both success and hardship.

The government and the people's concern for athletes and coaches has provided a favorable environment for them to bring their talents into full play. Schools and colleges are open to young athletes. With comfortable remuneration, the coaches lead a secure life. They enjoy reliable social security and will never become slaves of money. The Chinese government and the people have given them high honor. Some have been honored with such titles as "Model Worker," "March 8 Red Banner Bearer," "National Shock Worker

Chinese athletes such as world badminton champion Yang Yang receive great respect in their country.

in the New Long March," "Best Athlete," and others. Some have been elected national and local people's deputies, members of political consultative conferences, and leading members of Youth League Committees or Women's Federations.

The state has also conferred "Honor Medals" on world champions and world record breakers and First, Second, and Third Class Sports Medals on national champions and national record breakers. So far, more than 900 outstanding athletes and sports workers have received such medals.

Chinese athletes and coaches always live up to the care and the honor they are given. In competition, they follow the moral code of "fair competition and group endeavor" and never hesitate to dedicate their wisdom and energy to scaling new peaks. In daily life, they demonstrate outstanding citizenship. Many famous athletes and coaches have raised money to set up sports foundations. Some have contributed large sums for the development of the nation's physical education and to reward those who have made contributions in training athletes.

When athletes reach the end of their competitive careers, they often become either coaches or officials in their sports. Others engage in scientific research or write books. Even the handicapped try to make themselves useful to society. One example is Hu Zurong, a national record breaker, in pole vault. He became paralyzed as a result of an injury during training. Without losing hope, he began writing, and, after overcoming numerous difficulties with painstaking efforts, published two books: *Fourteen Hundred Demonstrations in Physical Training* and *Pole Vault*. His story represents the noble quality of Chinese athletes.

Experts Who Develop World Champions

An old Chinese saying goes: Jade is not of much use before it is carved. Likewise, good athletes cannot grow without expert coaches who can identify and nurture them into world champions. China's coaches come from three sources: former athletes, graduates of sports colleges, and amateur sports fans.

A Look at Successful Coaches

China has had three world record breakers in the high jump. One is Zheng Fengrong, who broke the world record in women's high jump in 1957; another is Ni Zhiqin, who set the world record in men's high jump in 1970. The man who made them world record breakers is Huang Jian, their coach. Huang fell in love with sports as a child. After graduating from the Moscow Institute of Physical Training in 1951, he returned to China. In 1953, he discovered the promising Zheng Fengrong at the National Sports Meet. Thereafter, he began to teach her the scissor-type jumping technique, which he felt was best suited to her physique. In 1957, Zheng jumped over 1.77 meters, setting a new world record in the women's high jump. Never sticking to conventions, Huang Jian used different methods to train Ni Zhiqin and Zheng Dazhen, making the former a world record holder and the latter an Asian female record holder.

Huang pays attention to practice, respects science, and continues to explore new summits of high jumping. One cannot talk about China's achievements in the high jump without mentioning Huang's contribution.

Hu Hongfei, the coach of Zhu Jianhua, who has three times broken world records, was an amateur long- and medium-distance runner and an English teacher before becoming a highly sophisticated and successful coach. In the 1960s, he trained Xuan Xiaomei to be a national record holder of women's high jump. Starting in 1972, he began to train Zhu Jianhua in the light of his new theory, "speed + technique = height." In less than 10 years, he helped Zhu break the world record.

Under his coach's guidance, Zhu Jianhua (holding flowers) established three world records in the high jump in 1983.

Many other renowned coaches, including Yuan Weimin, Xu Yinsheng, and Li Furong, have gone through extraordinary experiences and contributed prodigiously to China's physical culture. If we describe China's outstanding athletes as a cluster of bright stars, we can depict the excellent coaches as rosy clouds shining in brilliance. They mount the world sports arena together with their champions. Some have appeared on the prize-giving platforms, but most never have. However, they deserve the same honor because they have also contributed much to the success of China's athletes.

Coaches Abroad

Chinese coaches play an increasingly important role in promoting world sports. The number of Chinese coaches working in foreign countries has jumped from 100 in 1980 to over 300 today. In the past decade, China sent over 1,000 coaches to 67 countries and regions, including both developing and developed countries. In 1986, 42 countries in Asia, Africa, Europe, and the Americas invited Chinese coaches specializing in 15 events including table tennis, gymnastics, and volleyball. In the sport of table tennis alone, since 1959 China has sent 412 coaches to other countries, 54 of whom are now still working overseas. The coaches sent abroad in 1986 came from national teams, sports institutes, and various trade athletic associations in 28 provinces, autonomous regions, and municipalities directly under the central government. The contingent of Chinese coaches overseas is rapidly expanding.

Chinese coaches working abroad have been well received for their hard work and strong skills. As a result, more and more countries have extended coaching contracts or increased invitations. The number of Chinese coaches invited by Arab countries, for instance, rose from 57 in 1980 to 116 in 1986. Su Shiyao, a gymnastics coach working in Kuwait, was asked to stay for 9 years. Su was thus called the "father of gymnastics" in Kuwait.

Huang Zhiyuan, a badminton coach on loan to Singapore, was named "super coach" because his strict training program helped send Singapore's national team to the quarterfinal during the qualification competition for the Thomas Cup.

Under the training of Chinese coach Bu Zhuangxia, the Italian women's volleyball team qualified for the World Women's Volleyball Tournament for the first time and gained ninth place. Later, it beat Japan to come in fourth during an international women's volleyball match in which eight countries participated. Bu won the Italian Volleyball Association's praise and trust and was appointed general coach of the Italian Women's Team.

Efforts to Improve

Compared with major world sports powers, both the quantity and quality of the Chinese coaches still need to improve. Currently, there are over 26,000 professional coaches in China, 1,378 of whom have obtained titles of various grades, including 358 senior coaches. Since the founding of the People's Republic, China's sports organizations have attached great importance to fostering coaches and improving their competence. A series of regulations and systems have been formulated in this regard. The "Draft Regulations for the Work of Sports Teams" clearly stipulates the responsibilities of coaches. They include these: The coaches must try to raise their political consciousness and professional expertise; a grade system shall be instituted for coaches; and departments or specialties for training coaches shall be established in sports colleges. Since the beginning of the 1980s, the state and provincial physical culture and sports commissions have opened new channels and adopted a series of new measures to train coaches. In 1981, the State Physical Culture and Sports Commission authorized the sports colleges in Beijing, Shanghai, and Tianjin to establish training courses for coaches. Since 1983, sports colleges in Beijing, Shanghai, Wuhan, Shenyang, Xi'an, and Chengdu have offered correspondence courses for coaches. As a result, 1,161 coaches have been trained since 1981.

The educational level of the 4,300 coaches for top sports teams has also changed: Since 1981, the proportion of coaches that have university or college education has risen from 19% to 46%. In addition, some sports colleges now offer short-term refresher or training courses for coaches of junior spare-time sports schools. The State Physical Culture and Sports Commission made it clear in 1986 that, by the year 1990, coaches of all the top sports teams should acquire university or college degrees, and that those under 40 who do not have college diplomas should devote 5 years to study. Should they fail to obtain diplomas in 5 years, they will be disqualified for coaching. Professional titles are conferred strictly in accordance with the academic requirements set out by the state.

Along with seniority and work achievements, academic records are one of the important standards for testing, job assignments, and promotion. Coaches for national and provincial intensive training teams are selected according to the recommendations of related individual sports event associations, and associate coaches are named by the chief coaches. The above-mentioned rules and regulations are producing a positive and far-reaching influence on the professional competence of China's coaches.

Summary

Only recent entrants to the international sporting scene, Chinese athletes have produced spectacular results during the past 30 years. Chinese athletes have won numerous world championships and Olympic medals and have set many world records. The rapid attainment of excellence by a nation that shunned international competition through the 1960s is a tribute to the dedication of China's young athletes, the skill of their coaches, and the organization of China's sport system.

Modern Sports Sciences and Sports Medicine

P
A
R
T

I
I

Though research in sports medicine and sports science was initiated shortly after the establishment of the People's Republic of China in 1949, major research efforts and resources were not extended until the period between the mid-1950s and early 1960s. Then the Cultural Revolution closed research institutes and academic institutions through most of the period from 1966 to 1976 and brought research to a virtual standstill. However, since the beginning of the Period of Reform in the late 1970s, great strides have been taken toward producing better personnel, facilities, equipment, and programs. Chapters 9 through 13 present the development, organization, major research findings, and goals of sports medicine and the sports sciences against the backdrop of these political events.

Photo on facing page: Many tests are conducted on athletes at the National Research Institute of Sports Science in Beijing.

Chapter 9

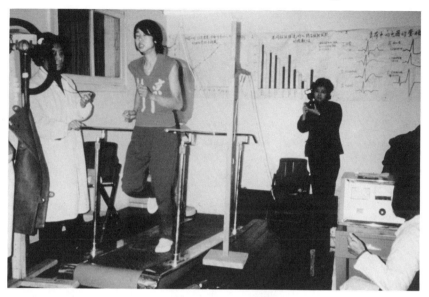

Scientific Research in Physical Education and Sport

YANG Tianle

Formal scientific research in China did not begin until the 20th century. To understand the present state of China's sport-related research, the history of China's scientific research must be investigated. China has established an effective research system, consisting of institutions and organizations. Considering the setback of the Cultural Revolution, researchers have achieved much in the areas of physical education and sports, and Chinese scientists have set specific goals for future research emphasis.

History of Scientific Research in Physical Education and Athletics

Planned, scientific physical education research started in various countries as late as the early years of this century. It was considerably developed after World War II. In China, from the 1930s until the founding of People's Republic in 1949, the foundation of scientific research work on physical education was very weak, although some academic articles were published. Almost no experimental research was conducted during this period. There was no research organization. Formal research started only after 1949.

The Start of Formal Research Work

In 1954, a postgraduate school for the study of physical education and sports was established at the Central Physical Education and Athletic College. Experts from the Soviet Union were invited as tutors, and physical education and athletic research work started.

The first physical education and athletics research organization in China was established in 1958 as the Beijing Physical Education and Athletic Research Institute. In 1972, the name was subsequently changed to the National Research Institute of Sports Science. Most of the original research workers were graduates of academic programs in the Soviet Union and Hungary. The first section set up was the Medical and Physiology Research Section, followed by the Physical Education Theories and Teaching Methods Section. In the following year, the Institute of Sports Medicine was established at Beijing Medical College, which is now called Beijing Medical University. In the 1960s, many other research organizations were established all over the country. There were the Shanghai and Heilongjiang Physical Education and Athletic Research Institutes, Guandong Province Commission of Physical Education and Athletic Office, Research Section of History of Physical Education and Athletics and Sports Medicine at Chengdu, and the Physical Education and Athletic College in Sichuan province. For promoting the exchange of information, many periodicals were also established during that period.

In 1960, the first National Physical Education and Athletic Research Conference was held. Among the topics discussed were training, physiology, and biochemistry in physical education and athletics, anatomy, nutrition, sports injuries, and medical supervision. Such traditional Chinese events as taijiquan and qigong were also discussed.

In December 1964, the first National Academic Conference of Physical Education and Athletics was held. The purpose of the conference was to exchange information and compare the accomplishments and experiences of different organizations. There were 126 formal representatives and 350 auditors

Chinese sport scientists can draw on ancient as well as modern exercise techniques in their research.

participating, and 321 theses from 82 organizations of 22 districts were collected. After being carefully appraised, 109 papers were presented during the conference, and 91 were published for distribution. Some were considered to be of great value. These included such studies as "The Change of Some Functions of Human Body at High Altitude—Hypoxic Conditions and Their Application"; "The Change of Body Mechanics of Soccer Players During Competition or Heavy Load Training"; "The Research of Prevention and Treatment of Athletic Injuries"; and "Methods of Achieving Speed Stamina in Soccer Player Training."

The Cultural Revolution (1966-1976) resulted in the closing of all research institutions and the dismissal of research staff. All physical education and athletic research work ceased.

Physical education and athletic research resumed in 1976 and it was listed in the "National Project of Developing Science and Technology" by the State Commission of Science and Technology in 1978. Thereafter, many physical education and athletic research organizations were established or reestablished and research staffs reorganized in provinces, autonomous regions, municipalities, and physical education colleges.

The Second Conference of Scientific and Technical Physical Education and Athletics was held in May 1979. Emphasis was on the discussion of establishing and strengthening organizations and identifying needs for research. At the same time, new trends for international physical education and athletic research were also discussed.

Recent Development

The 1980s brought a period of new development. Research institutions developed and the contingent of research workers enlarged. More than 20 new research institutes were established, including Kunming Physical Education Electrical Facilities Research Institute, Chengdu Sport Medicine Research Institute, and other research organizations in provinces and municipalities including Beijing, Jilin, Jiangsu, Jiangxi, Gansu, and Guangxi. By the end of 1986, there were 31 institutions with 1,400 research workers.

An Association of the Science of Physical Education and Athletics was established in 1980. A periodical named *Science of Physical Education and Athletics* was published. Another periodical named *China Sport Medicine* began publication in 1982. Both of these magazines are quarterlies and are issued for both Chinese and foreigners. There are abstracts written in English for all published academic articles.

There has also been tremendous development in international academic exchange. Chinese physical education and athletic scientific workers have participated in numerous international conferences and meetings including meetings on international sports medicine, biomechanics, sport psychology, sports biochemistry, comparative physical education, the Olympic Science Conference, the Asian Physical Education and Athletic Science Meeting, and sports medicine conferences in the United States, Japan, and the German Democratic Republic. There were also study groups sent to Europe, America, Japan, and Australia to study physical education and athletic research work and strengthen cooperation with these countries. Meanwhile, China has invited many physical education and athletic scholars from different countries to China to present lectures and participate in academic conferences. It is especially worthy to point out that in 1980, a relationship between the Chinese Association of Sports Medicine and the American College of Sports Medicine (ACSM) was established. A number of ACSM officers came to China for activities of exchange and to present lectures (e.g., H. Montoy, H.G. Knuttgen, L. Micheli, D.R. Lamb, H. Miller, and J. Bergfeld). Starting in 1981, Professor Knuttgen (Pennsylvania State University) visited China seven times to present lectures and participate in academic conferences. These visits have significantly aided the exchange of views regarding physical education and sports medicine.

In November 1984, the third session of the National Physical Education Science and Technology Steering Conference was held. The policy of development of physical education science and technology was affirmed. It was agreed that the development of physical education and athletics depended on the progress of such science and technology.

Research System for Physical Education and Sports

With the philosophical and financial support of the government, a number of major research institutes and organizations have been established throughout China during the past 30 years. A description of this system follows.

The State Physical Education and Sports Commission.   This commission is the national overseeing body for physical education and sports research. Under its direct leadership are four research institutes engaged in full-time research work and six institutes of physical education (see Figure 9.1) each of which has a scientific research bureau responsible for organization, coordination, and administration of research. The budgets of these units are provided by the national government.

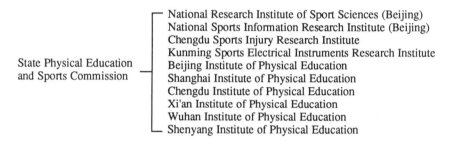

State Physical Education and Sports Commission

- National Research Institute of Sport Sciences (Beijing)
- National Sports Information Research Institute (Beijing)
- Chengdu Sports Injury Research Institute
- Kunming Sports Electrical Instruments Research Institute
- Beijing Institute of Physical Education
- Shanghai Institute of Physical Education
- Chengdu Institute of Physical Education
- Xi'an Institute of Physical Education
- Wuhan Institute of Physical Education
- Shenyang Institute of Physical Education

Figure 9.1   Organizations overseen by the State Physical Education and Sports Commission.

Institutes belonging to provinces, municipalities, and autonomous regions. There are 27 full-time institutions and 8 colleges in which research work is conducted. Figure 9.2 shows this breakdown. (The term *normal universities* refers to teacher education universities.)

The State Education Commission.   This commission is responsible for school physical education and athletic research work (see Figure 9.3). There are physical education departments at various universities for teacher education. Certain universities have established research institutes, but all normal universities and colleges have physical education and athletic sections.

Ministry of Health.   The Ministry oversees much of the research on sports medicine. Figure 9.4 illustrates divisions of the medical colleges and universities under the Ministry's supervision.

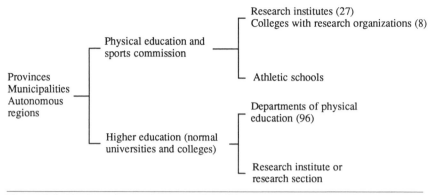

Figure 9.2   Institutes in provinces, municipalities, and autonomous regions conducting research.

Figure 9.3   Areas overseen by the State Education Commission.

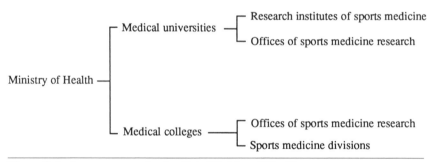

Figure 9.4   Areas overseen by the State Ministry of Health.

National physical education and sport associations of China.   A number of research committees exist in the various athletic associations responsible for organizing and promoting research pertaining to specific athletic events. Budgets for these committees are granted by their respective associations and then used to conduct various research projects.

Among all the organizations listed, the State Physical Education and Sports Commission possesses the most advanced research facilities and prominent research workers. Its main tasks are raising the levels of specific athletic events and applying basic principles of science to physical education and athletics. Meanwhile, the problems of improving the physical status of Chinese people as a whole have not been overlooked. The Physical Education and Sports Commission now has 207 research workers devoted to this problem, including 25 senior members with the rank of associate professor or higher and 90 engineers and lecturers.

Among these distinguished researchers, four are in the standing Committee of the Chinese Association of Physical Education and Athletics, in which there are 19 members elected from such national associations as the Chinese Association of Athletic Training, Chinese Association of Sports Medicine, Chinese Association of Athletic Biomechanics, Chinese Association of Athletic Information, Chinese Research Institute of Athletic Equipment and Facilities, and the National Research Institute of Sports Science. All these members hold offices in the aforementioned organizations.

The National Research Institute of Sports Science, the first sports science institute in the People's Republic of China, was established on September 18, 1958, in Beijing. The Institute has the dual role of carrying out basic research and training postgraduate students in the various areas of sports science. Postgraduate training is provided in sports medicine, physiology of exercise, sports biomechanics, athletic training, and sports information, and the students receive master's degrees on graduation. This institution has established formal relationships with corresponding organizations and experts in more than 20 countries. Administratively, the institute is made up of eight departments, a central laboratory, a sports information and documentation section, and a film and video studio. The eight departments are listed here:

- Athletic training
- Ball games training (including a sport psychology section)
- Sports biomechanics
- Mass sports
- Sports medicine
- Exercise physiology
- Sports theory
- Sports instrumentation

Training Research Workers

With the closing of institutions of education and research during the Cultural Revolution (1966-1976), scientists engaged in physical education and sport research lost much valuable time and experience. A 10-year lapse in the recruitment and training of young scientists resulted in a significant age gap in such personnel. Consequently, present-day research laboratories and institutes are staffed by personnel trained either before or after the Cultural Revolution.

Period of Soviet Influence (1954-1960)

After the establishment of a graduate school at the Central Physical Education and Athletic College in 1954, Soviet instructors were invited each year to teach courses of physiology of exercise, athletic anatomy, medical care, principles of physical education and athletics, and specific sports events such as swimming, gymnastics, and track-and-field. A group of research workers was trained in research techniques. Also, a group of selected students and postgraduates were recommended for admission to study in the Soviet Union and Hungary. Among these students, six obtained doctoral degrees. This group soon became the backbone of sports research work in China and established the foundation for future research. However, the Soviet system did not fit the Chinese situation very well.

Source of Sports Research Personnel

Full-time sports research personnel are mainly recipients of master's and doctoral degrees from the Physical Education and Athletic Research Institute and various colleges of physical education and athletics. Others are college graduates with excellent academic records from departments of basic science, such as physiology of exercise, biochemistry, anatomy, biomechanics, and sports medicine. Others are from the Department of Physical Education and Athletics, Department of Sports Medicine, at the College of Physical Education and Athletics in Chengdu. Some are graduates of comprehensive universities and universities of technology, medicine, and natural sciences. There are also postgraduate students who majored in corresponding subjects and some experienced former coaches. These people are all knowledgeable about basic principles of physical education and athletics. The latter groups perform mainly research work in athletic training. Qiu Zhonghui is an outstanding example. The first Chinese world champion of table tennis, she is now conducting research on the training of table tennis athletes.

Needs for the Future

Reviewing the past 30 years, we find the following:

- While a mastery of basic principles and fundamental skills has been accomplished, new scientific knowledge and skills must be acquired.
- Research workers must be enthusiastic about and familiar with sports. For example, those devoted to sports training research must work directly with athletes in their actual training.
- Sports researchers should know at least one foreign language so they

can learn from the experience of other countries. Multilingualism facilitates academic exchange with research workers of other countries.

- It is important to produce researchers with firm political commitment as well as initiative, ambition, diligence, vigor, and dedication to learning.
- Attention should be paid to the training of leaders. Promising individuals should be presented with opportunities to obtain special learning, including studying or visiting abroad.

Main Achievements in Sports Research

Since 1917, physical education and athletics in China has stepped into a period of rapid development. It would take lengthy reports to describe all the achievements in the research areas of sports medicine, physiology of exercise, sports biochemistry, biomechanics, and sport psychology. However, some achievements in other areas are introduced in the following sections.

Studies Regarding Mass Sports and People's Health

In 1980, the physique, motor ability, and physical condition of large numbers of teenagers and children in 16 locations throughout China, including

International exchange facilitates advancement for sports scientists.

provinces, municipalities, and autonomous regions, were studied by more than 1,500 research workers and school teachers. Fully 4,401,936 data were recorded from a 23-item test given to 183,414 students in 1,210 universities, secondary schools, and elementary schools. Based on these data, the present condition and characteristics of young people's physique were studied and standards of evaluation of growth, motor ability, and quality of physique were made for different age groups. This research has proved to be extremely valuable as a reference for school education, medical care, and physical education in China. This research achievement has been granted not only the Science Technology Awards of National and Ministry grade, but also the Honorable Athletic Award by the national government.

In 1982, a study was conducted to standardize age grouping and grading for The National Athletic Training Standards. Research workers and school teachers collected and investigated information about the physiques and motor abilities of 90,000 students from 200 universities, secondary schools, and elementary schools in different provinces, municipalities, and autonomous regions. Statistical analysis was accomplished for 750,000 recorded data from indexes of 25 athletic items. This study resulted in the publication of the National Athletic Training Standards, providing a valuable scientific basis for developing and improving school physical education and mass sports.

Criteria for Selecting Athletes

For many years, athletes were selected through the intuition and experience of coaches. A major national project was undertaken in the early 1980s that resulted in the publication of a report, "Research of Selecting Promising Youngster Athletes." It was completed through the cooperation of several institutions between 1980 and 1982. Participating were the Athletic Research Institute of the State Physical Education and Sports Commission; the Sports Research Institutes of Shanghai, Beijing, Guangdong, Liaoning, and Gansu; and the Colleges of Physical Education and Athletics of Shanghai, Beijing, and Wuhan. There were 123 research articles published discussing the criteria and standards of reference for evaluating and selecting promising athletes, along with theoretical considerations. These articles were based on more than 748,000 original data recorded during the testing of 102 items covering body form, quality, functional ability, psychological condition, and heredity. Among the 14,871 persons tested were prominent athletes in five sports: track-and-field, swimming, gymnastics, volleyball, and soccer. Included were world champions and the six best performers in competitive events in national competitions. Other participants were drawn from spare-time athletic school students from elementary and secondary schools. The research had great significance for identifying and training prospective athletes. Its results and recommendations have been adapted for application by many provinces and municipalities; the success these provinces and municipalities have had in selecting their athletes has increased markedly. The research won the First-Class Science-Technology Progress Award given by the State Physical Education and Sports Commission in 1985.

Raising Sports Skill Levels Through Training Techniques

Recently, Chinese researchers have begun to apply sports research to improve athletes' skills. The sports of sprinting and table tennis have benefited from this research.

Sprinting

Based on systems engineering approaches to research, the national sprinting team runners have been studied by the cooperative activities of coaches and research workers during their training programs.

During the course of a 3-year research program, the sprinters achieved excellent results, breaking the Asian records in the men's 100-meter dash and the 4x100-meter relay. The two records remain unbroken to the present. These records contributed to the fame China received when winning such a large number of gold medals during the 10th Asian Athletic Meet in 1986.

Table Tennis

Research on table tennis was conducted by a group of 10 research workers and well known table tennis coaches. Effective ways of improving the training of the five principal elements of table tennis (accuracy, speed, strength, spin, and placement) were explained through the application of the knowledge of mechanics, physiology, and the combination of theory and practice. The research project identified and described 10 distinct styles of playing, 20 methods of serving the ball, and 214 individual skill techniques. The characteristics of all skills and the quality requirements were meticulously analyzed. This research achievement had great theoretical significance and value for the development of this sport in China and elsewhere.

Application of Modern Scientific Knowledge and Techniques

The rapid development of modern science and technology in China has extended into its sports research. Electronic technology, telemetry, and advanced optics and acoustics have been applied to the construction of sports facilities and equipment, with important implications for athletes. The following are some of the more important developments:

- Electronic computers that analyze volleyball skills and tactics
- A new instrument, the YJ-B swimming relay race tester, that effectively solves the longstanding problem of analyzing the swimming relay

Research in table tennis has played a major role in the success of China's national team during the past twenty years.

- A rapid retrieval data system regarding the characteristics of athletic skills
- Eight-channel electromyographical telemeters
- Computerized speed testing instruments
- Photographic athletic skill analysis instruments
- Table tennis ball-shooting machines
- MB-II pulse hydraulic massage machines
- Electronic facilities used in track-and-field meets

Scientific and Technological Intelligence in Sport

Intelligence (or information processing) is an important aspect in sports organization. This area has developed rapidly during the past few years in China. A great amount of work has been accomplished in such aspects of information processing as information collection, transfer, analysis, and dissemination. The information concerned involves technique, theory, method, and research of strategy of athletic development. The latest information offered has produced highly positive effects on athletic policy-making, management, training, teaching, and research. The following are the main achievements.

Chinese Sports in A.D. 2000

This research project analyzed the social function of sports and examined the strategy of development of sports in China. A forecast for the future of physical education and sports and for sports science and technology in China was then made. This achievement constitutes a valuable reference for identifying national projects and has proven useful in the development of a national strategy of sport enhancement.

Spiking Skills and Tactics of Famous Volleyball Spikers

The skills and tactics of "spiking"—in which a player strikes the ball overhand into the opposing team's court—was studied using both American and Japanese volleyball players. The following items were analyzed: techniques of spiking used by different players at different attacking spots; characteristics of spiking; changes of spiking direction; and ball-dropping (dinking) techniques. The research results were presented to the Chinese national women's volleyball team to help both coaches and players plan strategy and develop drills. The results helped the players improve their abilities to make quick decisions during competition. This research has undoubtedly contributed greatly to the success of Chinese women's volleyball.

Organization of Olympic Programs

Information obtained from the Soviet Union, the United States, the German Democratic Republic, and Cuba about their Olympic programs was studied and analyzed for the purpose of establishing general guidelines. The suggestions obtained helped in organizing the Chinese Olympic program. This research work is of theoretical and practical significance in achieving better results with limited personnel, finances, and physical material.

Present Orientation of Sports and Physical Education Research

The continued popularization of sports among the people for their health requires further research work. The enhancement of the competitive levels of China's elite athletes depends more than ever on the guidance and coordination provided by research. There are many problems in both mass and competitive sports waiting to be solved. With limited expertise and budget, main objectives had to be chosen and priorities clearly defined. Considering the needs of the entire nation, the following ten items were selected by the State Physical Education and Sports Commission for emphasis in future research:

- Physical status (physique) of the Chinese population, including that of pupils and students of all grades, laborers, and office workers
- Chinese boxing and breathing exercises, which are valuable athletic heritages of China
- Procedures for selection of promising young athletes

- Analysis of skills of athletes; evaluation of motor ability and psychological training
- Athletes' nutrition, nourishing drugs, and methods for eliminating fatigue
- Improved performance and competitive results in track-and-field, swimming, and soccer
- Examination of the application of excitatory drugs
- The application of electronic computers to sports
- Establishment of an information system for modern sports
- Development of sports equipment and facilities

These 10 items all involve major problems and concern knowledge of many scientific subjects. Obviously sports research workers cannot complete such a task alone. It will be necessary to interact with research staffs in many other areas, such as education, health, natural sciences, and technology. At the same time, it is necessary to draw on the resources of the National Athletic Association and its 12 branch committees.

Summary

Chinese scientists are striving to regenerate the research programs suspended during the Cultural Revolution and to initiate new programs. By their own initiative and through contacts and exchange with scientists from other countries, Chinese scientists are establishing physical education and sport research in China at an international level of quality. By hosting scientific meetings for visiting international scientists and by participating in meetings and congresses around the world, China is fueling the fires of sport science research. These contributions have profoundly impacted physical education and sport science in China.

Photo on facing page: Small containers that apply suction are used in traditional Chinese medicine for the treatment of a lower back problem.

Chapter 10

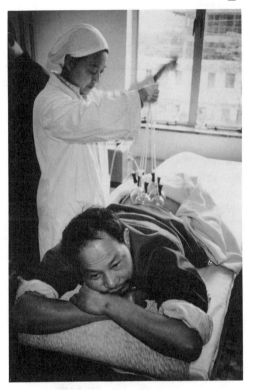

Sports Medicine

WENG Qingzhang

Like the sports sciences, sports medicine in China was not extensively researched until after 1949. Since the founding of the People's Republic, China has established several sports medicine organizations and has made great gains in research and in training research workers and team physicians in sports medicine.

Recent History of Sports Medicine

Because sports in China were still undeveloped before 1949, sports medicine was virtually nonexistent during that time. In the beginning of the 1950s, only a small number of physicians joined in the medical service of the national sports teams as they became organized. In 1956, however, Soviet medical experts were invited to Beijing to initiate training courses on sports medicine, including the topics of sports injuries, medical supervision of athletes, and physical therapy. Soviet academicians were also invited to the Beijing Institute of Physical Education to organize postgraduate training courses on sports physiology and functional anatomy. Several Chinese were sent as postgraduates to study sports medicine in the Soviet Union and Hungary. A Chinese research group was sent to the Soviet Union in 1957.

Since 1958, a number of sports medicine organizations have been established, specializing in research, injury prevention, and injury treatment. Those established earliest (under the State Physical Education and Sports Commission) were the Research Department of Sports Medicine and the Research Department of Sports Physiology at the National Research Institute of Sports Science; and the Institute of Sports Medicine at Beijing Medical University. This marked the formal beginning of research work on sports medicine in China.

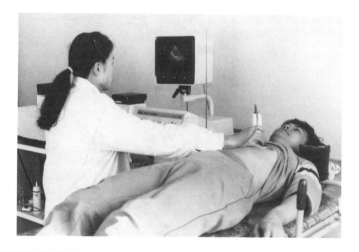

A sports medicine researcher uses ultrasound while examining an athlete.

During the late 1950s, prevention and treatment units for sports medicine were established in more than 10 medical colleges, with former students from the 1956 training course and the 1954 postgraduate training course as the key figures. Courses on sports medicine were also introduced at several colleges of physical education. A certain number of physicians were allocated to training centers for provincial and municipal sports teams.

The First Conference on Sports Science took place in 1964. It drew its participants from several research institutes. Faculty of several medical colleges and universities and team physicians from a number of sports teams presented dozens of papers concerning sports medicine and sports physiology. A preliminary national framework of prevention, treatment, and research on sports medicine was formed. This was largely the result of the lessons learned from Soviet and other Eastern European colleagues and constituted a significant event in the early development of sports medicine in China.

The development of sports medicine in China stood still during the Cultural Revolution of 1966-1976 and resumed gradually in the late 1970s. After a National Conference on Science and a National Conference on Physical Culture in 1978, physical education began to flourish again in China, and simultaneously, sports medicine entered a new stage of rapid development.

Organizations and Academic Exchange

Among the recently established provincial institutes for sports science throughout China, about one dozen were research departments of sports medicine. Courses on sports medicine for professional personnel were initiated in 10 institutes of physical culture and a few dozen normal colleges and universities of physical culture. Anywhere from 10 to 40 full-time medical workers were allocated to each of the training centers established for athletes in 29 provinces and municipalities.

The Chinese Association of Sports Medicine was established in 1978 and became a member of the International Federation of Sports Medicine (FIMS) in 1980. The election of a new slate of officers took place in May 1985, when six different professional groups were organized under the Association: Sports Physiology, Sports Biochemistry and Nutrition, Sports Injuries, Medical Supervision, Physical Therapy, and Sports Anatomy. In September 1986, Qu Mianyu, president of the Association, was elected to a vice-presidency in FIMS on the occasion of the 23rd World Conference of Sports Medicine in Brisbaine, Australia.

By the end of 1986, 900 lecturers, visiting scientists, and assistant research fellows made up the membership of the Chinese Association of Sports Medicine. In addition, there were also 400 medical workers of lesser credentials who were involved with the Association but did not qualify for membership. A number of activities of exchange of information and expertise were established both inside China and with foreign countries.

Since 1979, there has been at least one national academic conference on sports medicine each year, either of a comprehensive nature or dealing with a single subject. In addition, many provincial or regional academic meetings take place on a regular basis. Scores of experts and scholars from more than 20 foreign countries have visited China to present lectures and engage in activities of exchange. More than 10 delegations of Chinese investigators have been sent to Western Europe, Eastern Europe, Japan, and Australia. Hundreds of students have been sent to the United States, West Germany, Japan, Canada, and Australia for advanced training or postgraduate study. In 1985, China conducted the First Beijing International Conference on Sports Medicine. Eighty-two foreign scholars from 16 countries participated in the conference.

In order to promote academic exchange on sports medicine and the development of health services in physical culture, the Chinese Association of Sports Medicine began publishing the *Chinese Journal of Sports Medicine*. Originally a quarterly publication, the journal expanded to six issues per year in 1988 and presently has a circulation of over 8,000. The journal is sent to more than 20 countries. Since 1984, summaries of all articles in the journal have been translated into English and sent to the Canadian International Information Center of Physical Education.

Training Research Workers and Physicians in Sports Medicine

Research personnel in sports medicine are drawn from recent graduates of medical colleges or practicing physicians with hospital experience. The Chinese Association of Sports Medicine is responsible for the organization of special short-term training programs, preparation of teaching materials, and didactic lectures and practical programs. Various methods are employed to train sports medicine personnel. These include the following:

- One year of professional training in sports medicine, generally in medical colleges on units dealing with injury prevention and treatment.
- Short-term training courses of 3 to 6 months dealing with a single subject, such as sports injuries, medical supervision of athletes, biochemistry and nutrition, or physical therapy. These courses are conducted by the Chinese Association of Sports Medicine, organized every year or two for groups of approximately 50 students.
- Key research institutes are appointed to accept 5 to 10 students to study for master's degrees in sports medicine.
- Students are sent abroad for anywhere from 3 months to one year to study such topics as arthroscopy.
- Lectures by visiting foreign experts are presented several times each year. On such occasions research workers and team physicians are assembled from local organizations or from all over China.

- Short-term (3 months) and long-term (1 year) professional training courses are offered to Chinese personnel by the Chinese Association of Sports Medicine. Personnel study at relevant organizations to acquire professional training in order to update their knowledge about such topics as traditional Chinese medicine, Chinese drugs, diagnosis of cardiovascular diseases, radioimmunity, and electron microscopy.

Team physicians for China's Olympic teams are selected from the medical staffs of training centers. Physicians selected usually have more practical experience and have a record of success in treating sports injuries.

Provincial team physicians are generally selected from the medical staffs of provincial training centers. Lower level sport teams generally have no special team physicians. The injured players are sent to and treated by outpatient departments of local hospitals. During official tournaments involving lower level teams, national or provincial team physicians are invited.

The organizing committee of all official competitions, regardless of the age of the competitors, establishes a medical department, which is responsible for emergency treatment of injured athletes. Usually, the injured athlete is sent to the clinical departments of surgery or osteology first and then referred to the appropriate department of sports medicine for further treatment. Depending on the type of injury, the injured athlete may be referred directly to the department of sports medicine for diagnosis and treatment.

Sports Medicine Research Papers

Since 1979, from 100 to 200 papers have been presented each year at the major academic/scientific meeting on sports medicine. During the past 8 years, over 1,200 papers have been presented, the important ones falling into the following four categories:

- Practical aspects of competitive sports
- Mechanisms and theory
- Application of new techniques
- Application of traditional medicine

Practical Aspects of Competitive Sports

Evaluation of the anaerobic threshold in cycling, track-and-field, and swimming athletes by means of blood lactic acid and respiratory exchange analysis. This helps coaches plan the training of different intensities for the individual athletes.

Exercise tests for the evaluation of athletes in different sports by means cycle ergometer, treadmill tests, step tests, and others.

General evaluation of overtraining using methods from various medical specialties including cardiology, neurology, and myology.

Measurement of telemetric heart rate and telemetric electrocardiogram during field and underwater exercises.

Study of the ultrasonic cardiogram and systolic time interval during exercise.

Sport drinks containing alkaline electrolytes and trace elements.

Diet and nourishment for athletes.

Measurement of heart and lung function during high altitude training for improving the endurance of the athletes.

Prediction of hypoxic endurance in mountaineers and simulation test at 9,500 meters altitude.

Twenty-year follow-up study of athletes with abnormal electrocardiograms.

Follow-up studies (5-23 years) of athletes with hypertension during motion.

Studies on hematuria and proteinuria in athletes.

Mechanisms and Theory

The use of muscle biopsy and electron microscopy techniques to observe the ultrastructure of the muscle in the study of delayed myalgia (delayed onset of muscle soreness). Marked changes were seen in the subcellular structures such as the myofibrils, mitochondria, and lysosomes.

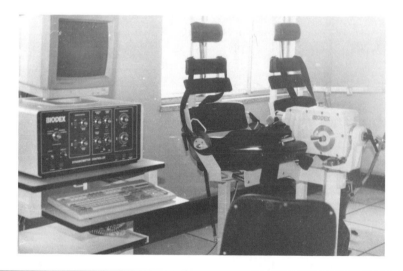

Contemporary research facilities throughout China such as the Research Center at the Beijing Institute of Physical Education employ modern testing equipment.

The treatment of *enthesiopathy*, which is a pathological change of the end structure of the patellar tendon. Degenerative changes of different degrees, such as necrosis of collagenous fibers and an inflammatory response of the surrounding tissue, occur at the end structure of the patellar tendon in athletes. Both the etiology of enthesiopathy structures and the effects of different drugs have been analyzed in the light of biomechanics. Animal experiments involving the use of cortisone, hyaluronidase, and Salvia Miltiorrhiza Bge (a Chinese medical herb that can enhance cardiac function) have proven helpful in treating this condition in clinical practice.

Animal models of tibia stress fracture in athletes.

Extracorporal culture and allografting of articular cartilage cells.

The study of motor nerve chemistry by means of metenkephalin radio-immunoassy.

Application of New Techniques

The influence of intensive physical condition on chromosomes.

Analysis of muscle electric potentials by means of electromyogram telemetry.

Cardiac output measurement as assisted by computer.

Twenty-four-hour continuous electrocardiogram.

Arthroscopic diagnosis and treatment.

Ultramicroanalysis of metabolic enzymes.

High frequency electrocardiology.

Computer analysis of the power spectrum of electroencephalography and visually induced potential.

Application of nuclear medicine techniques for early diagnosis of stress-induced bone injuries.

Application of Traditional Medicine

The integration of traditional Chinese and modern Western medicine to relieve fatigue, treat sports injuries, and improve athletic performance.

The effects of traditional Chinese herb drugs, such as Radix acanthopanacis senticosi, Panax pseudoginseng Wall, Notoginseng Hoo, Notoginseng Tseng, and Shengmaisan, in relieving sport-related fatigue.

The treatment of sports injuries with acupuncture.

Treating the protrusion of intervertebral discs by massage.

Animal experiments on the waiqi (outflowing energy) emitted during gigong breathing exercises.

Health effects of traditional wushu, power training, and calisthenic exercises.

The use of qigong and aerobic exercises in rehabilitative treatment of coronary artery disease.

Study on the mechanism and clinical application of massage and body manipulation.

Recommendations for Sports Medicine

The interaction among different branches of modern science has exerted a profound influence over the development of sports medicine. Therefore, future research should make full use of the various branches of medical science. For example, biomechanics must be taken into consideration in treating sports injuries; biochemistry should be used in the evaluation and medical supervision of athletes; and sport psychology should be considered in the overall estimation of whether an athlete is in good form. Only when such interdisciplinary goals have been accomplished can sports medicine in China make broader and deeper progress.

On-the-spot tests during training or even during competition should be increased, as these data most accurately reveal the load reaction of the organism and, when closely compared with laboratory tests and complemented with each other, may further the applicability of sports medicine toward the practice of training.

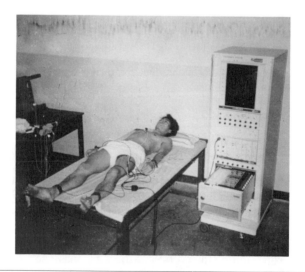

Regular testing and examination constitutes part of the medical and biological monitoring of an elite athlete.

Improvement of existing training methods and introduction of new techniques are important. The equipment for telemetering the electrocardiogram and the electromyogram needs further development. Techniques of telemetric electroencephalography should also be promoted. The study of computer treatment of bioelectric signals, automation and computerization of testing techniques, and the biochemical testing technique of microamounts of blood and other fluids (saliva, sweat, urine) should all be enhanced. Studies concerning sports physiology should be carried out based on ultramicromorphology and histochemistry of the tissues and on the level of cells and molecules so that the mechanism of the tissues may be better understood.

In treating sports injuries, modern transplantation materials and new techniques of repair should be adopted. For prevention of sports injuries, the problem of excess motion leading to injury should be studied.

Also, the contributions of traditional Chinese medicine and Chinese herbal drugs to sports medicine should be studied in depth. More studies should be conducted on the application and theories of fracture and dislocation reduction by Chinese orthopaedic techniques, the relief of fatigue by Chinese herbal drugs, and the prevention and treatment of sports injuries by massage and acupuncture.

With the increase in the quality of international sports competition and the great interest of Chinese people in physical fitness and general health, there are many new fields in sports medicine waiting for us to investigate.

Summary

Chinese sports medicine consists of a fascinating combination of traditional Chinese medicine and Western medicine. By exchanging medical literature, establishing dialogue with foreign physicians, and participating in international meetings, Chinese sports medicine personnel have shared their clinical and experimental results with others and profited from access to information from abroad. Recognizing these benefits, the Chinese Association of Sports Medicine and its members have become increasingly active internationally, strengthening its association with the International Federation of Sports Medicine (FIMS).

Photo on facing page: Research will benefit the masses as well as China's elite athletes.

Chapter 11

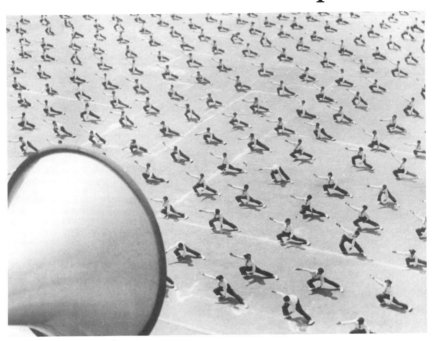

Recent Advances in Sports Physiology and Sports Biochemistry

YANG Zeyi

In international scientific circles, sports physiology found its beginnings in the 1930s while serious investigation of the biochemistry of sport reached maturity in the mid-1960s. When China's contact and exchange with foreign scientists began (after the Cultural Revolution), Chinese scientists made rapid progress and produced significant contributions to international sports physiology and biochemistry. From that time to the present, this trend of sport science advancement in China has only accelerated.

Development of Sports Physiology and Sports Biochemistry

Sports physiology as an independent branch of science was established in the 1950s in China, about 30 years later than in other nations. Before 1949, no work was done in this field except the book *Sports Physiology*, written by Cai Qiao in 1940. After the founding of the People's Republic of China, *Practical Sports Physiology*, written by Zhao Mingxue, was published in 1951. In 1954, the Department of Physiology of the Beijing Institute of Physical Education initiated classes and research work and enrolled the first group of 29 graduate students in this field.

At the same time, all the institutes of physical education in China began to include sports physiology in their curricula. In 1958, the National Research Institute of Sports Science was established, and the Department of Sports Physiology became its first research unit. In the 1950s and 1960s, a number of significant studies were completed, including the following: "The Establishment of Ready State by Verbal Strengthened Conditional Reflex" in 1956; "The Mechanism of Verbal Strengthened Sports Conditional Reflex" in 1958; "On the Problem of Fatigue" in 1960; "The Nature of Ready State" in 1961; "The Changes in Electroencephalogram During Experimental Fatigue" in 1963; and "The Changes in the Functions of Adrenal Cortex During Experimental Fatigue" in 1963. In 1964, a number of research papers were presented at the National Sports Science Symposium and the staff for teaching and research in this field was gradually increased in number.

The study of sports biochemistry began a little later than that on sports physiology. Classes on sports biochemistry in the colleges of physical education started in 1955, and research in this area started in 1958. A number of research achievements were attained in the early 1960s on topics such as the following: "Nutritional Status and Requirements of Vitamin C in the Gymnasts and Middle and Long Distance Runners"; "Preliminary Studies on the Water and Electrolyte Metabolism of Long Distance Runners in the Summer"; and "Preliminary Studies on the Effect of Sports on the Activity of Serum Transaminase."

Unfortunately, the political upheaval of the Cultural Revolution hindered the development of sports physiology and sports biochemistry for more than 10 years. In the last decade, however, significant advances have been made.

During the 4-year period from 1978 to 1982, the textbook *Sports Physiology*, uniformly used in physical education institutes throughout China, was reedited on two occasions. In 1983, the textbook *Sports Biochemistry* appeared.

Recent research in these two fields produced other important results. At the 1980 National Sports Science Academic Symposium, 69 papers were presented. In 1981 and 1983, national conferences on sports medicine were convened, during which 64 and 96 papers were presented, respectively. At the International Conference on Sports Medicine in Beijing in 1985, Chinese delegates presented 104 papers on sports physiology and sports biochemistry.

National conferences on sports physiology and biochemistry were convened in 1984 and 1986. In the 1984 conference, 133 papers were received and there were 183 participants. At the 1986 conference, the number of papers received and the number of participants rose to 232 and 293, respectively. By then, the methods of research, the fields of research, and the age distribution of the research workers were all in a better state of development.

Research Achievements in Sports Physiology

With the application of new experimental technology and methodology, progress in sports physiology has been greatly accelerated. Research is being conducted in almost every field connected with sports physiology. The major achievements are as follows:

Athletes' Hearts

The original methods used to study the hearts of athletes were electrocardiography and roentgenography. In 1960, the papers, "A Statistical Report on 200 Cases of ECG of Athletes," "Electrocardiograms of Chinese Marathon Runners," "An Analysis of Measurements Done on the X-ray Pictures of the Hearts of 300 Athletes," and "An Analysis of X-ray Pictures of the Hearts of 138 Athletes" were published. Since then, studies on the electroardiograms of athletes at rest and under different exercise conditions became popular. In 1981, the 24-hour continuous recording of electrocardiograms was first used, and it was shown that such monitoring was better than the exercise test for the diagnosis of cardiac arrhythmia.

Systolic time interval (STI) is a noninvasive test used in recent years to assess the left ventricular function of athletes. STI tests have been performed on athletes of different ages and different training levels both at rest and during recovery after exercise in order to determine the differences in cardiac function among them. It was shown that STI, especially STI during graded exercise testing, is an accurate method of assessing the cardiac function of athletes of different tolerance levels.

Echocardiography is another method used to study the hearts of athletes. Originally echocardiography was used for observations of subjects at rest, exploring such topics as the differences in heart function between athletes and nonathletes and comparisons between the effects different sports and different levels of training had on the heart. Now echocardiography is applied to observations of exercising subjects after different training regimens, the results of which can be used to assess the ventricular systolic function and other effects of sports on cardiac function. Starting in 1985, various investigators have used echocardiography in the study of the diastolic function of the left ventricle. They concluded that diastolic functional changes occurring before the systolic change can be accurately used in the assessment of the threshold of cardiac pathophysiology during physical training.

Besides the more commonly used methods of structural and functional studies stated above, phonocardiography, electroechocardiography, cardiac output metering, and apexcardiography have been used to study the hearts of athletes.

Athletes of all of China's national teams benefit from sports science research.

Aerobic and Anaerobic Metabolism and Physical Performance

The maximum oxygen intake ($\dot{V}O_2max$), as one of the effective indices of cardiopulmonary function and aerobic exercise capacity, is commonly used in the evaluation of the function and the training practice of athletes. As early as 1965, the paper, "An Exploration on the Methods of Measuring Maximum Oxygen Intake," was published. Since then many more papers in this field have appeared, including papers studying $\dot{V}O_2max$ levels of people engaged in different kinds of sports and under different exercise conditions. In order to simplify the method, some investigators studied the correlation between $\dot{V}O_2max$ and other methods of estimating aerobic energy cost.

The concept of anaerobic threshold (the exercise intensity at which muscle lactic acid level increases continuously) was introduced in sports physiology in recent years and studied by Chinese investigators. Many investigators hold that the increase of aerobic performance capacity of athletes is not only due to the increase of $\dot{V}O_2max$ but also to an elevation in the anaerobic threshold, the latter being accepted as even more important. The nature of a blood lactic acid "transformation point" as observed by Yang Kueshen and others in a field experiment in 1979 is close to that of the anaerobic threshold concept.

In recent years, there were reports on the relationships among arterial blood lactic acid, acetone, and blood gas changes before and after anaerobic threshold by Pu Juncong and others and a report on the anaerobic threshold test of 35 athletes by Liu Shanyun and others. It was shown by Weng Qingzhang and others that the blood lactic acid curve obtained after graded training was

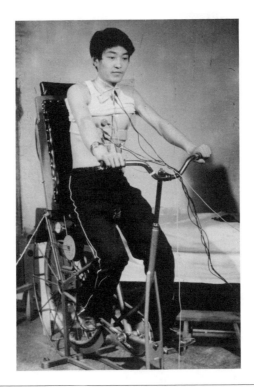

Elite athletes frequently serve as research subjects in physiological studies of human performance.

a better indication as to whether the aerobic and anaerobic capacities of athletes in different phases of training were elevated and, if so, to what extent. Weng found a close relationship between the increase of anaerobic capacity and the training achievements at the end of the training period.

Besides $\dot{V}O_2$max and anaerobic threshold, more simplified physiological methods for the assessment of aerobic and anaerobic capacity of athletes have also been developed. There are many reports on the use of the PWC_{170} functional test (a direct or indirect quantitative test for the determination of exercise tolerance of athletes when the intensity of physical exercise causes a heart rate of 170/min), single loading test (e.g., squat-and-rise-up 20 times in 30 sec, 15 sec x 3, running in place with maximum effort, Wingate anaerobic bicycle test, etc.), combined functional-loading test (consisting of 3 different time intervals with different loads), and so forth. Studies with a 3-minute stepladder test, different kinds of modified bicycle ergometer tests, and treadmill tests have been recently reported.

Effect of Physical Training on Skeletal Muscle

Studies on muscle physiology have been undertaken recently by Chinese researchers in sports physiology. The use of sophisticated methods from electronics, histology, and histochemistry has solved a number of mysteries about muscle and physical exercise, muscle fatigue, and the mechanism of recovery.

Surface electromyography has become an important means of studying the functions of human muscles because it is noninvasive and is computerized for automatic data analysis. During the 1980s there have been many reports in this field. In 1980, Guo Qingfang and Yin Yinquing reported that the amplitude of the surface electromyogram (IEMG or RMS) was increased during muscular fatigue. In 1983, Zhow Shi showed that a significant elevation in the ratio of electromyopotential/muscular tension (E/T) could accurately reflect muscular fatigue. Other investigators showed that fatigue produced a shift to the left of the elctromyopotential spectrum (an increase of low-frequency constituents and a decrease of high-frequency constituents).

Guo Qinfang and colleagues used elecromyography to study the early occurrence of muscular soreness after training. It was found that early muscular soreness may be due to the fact that fatigue raises the excitability of the muscular sensory system (muscle spindles), causing the fatigued muscles to be maintained in a state of prolonged contraction (spasm), thus obstructing the local circulation.

In another study, Wang Nan used the correlation between surface electromyographic data (together with other parameters) and muscle fiber-type population to establish a regression equation by which nontraumatic determination of muscle-fiber type (slow-twitch and fast-twitch) was made possible.

The biopsy technique for the study of human muscle was introduced in the

1980s. Research on muscle has made rapid progress although there were not many papers in this field. Tao Xinming and colleagues, utilizing computerized tomography, biopsy, and histochemistry, found a way to differentiate an athlete's muscle fibers into types I & II, determine their distribution, their average surface area, and the quantity of fibers. In 1986, these investigators demonstrated that the hypertrophy of muscles after training depended upon the hypertrophy of individual muscle fibers. Zhou Qian studied the relationship between the composition of muscle fiber types I and II and the lactic acid anaerobic threshold and found that the elevation of the lactic acid anaerobic threshold was influenced by the fiber type population. This finding provided an important criterion for the selection of candidates for endurance sports.

In recent years some investigators studied the ultramicrostructures of skeletal muscle in an effort to explain the mechanism of recovery methods, particularly with reference to the traditional Chinese sports medicine techniques of acupuncture and qigong. It was discovered that acupuncture can significantly decrease the disorderly arrangement, ruptures, and foci of lysis of myofibrils, delaying onset of muscle soreness, and elevate the pain threshold. Animal experiments have shown that qigong waiqi (energy eminating from the body) on overexercised muscles of rabbits had the same effects as acupuncture.

Besides the research work in the three main fields of sports physiology presented, preliminary studies on electroencephalography, skeletal circulation, circulation to the limbs, and the body composition of athletes have also begun.

Research Achievements in Sports Biochemistry

Studies in sports biochemistry started somewhat late in China, but progress has been rapid in the last decade. Modern biochemical technology enables us to observe the minute changes in the inner environment and the metabolism of an organism so to accurately assess its functional state. Such work can provide a basis for scientific training and can reveal nutritional and pharmacological methods for enhancing the abilities of athletes. The major studies on sports biochemistry carried out recently in China are as follows.

Ergogenic Aids in Sports

In modern competitive sports, victory or failure often depends upon a difference of one centimeter or one one-thousandth of a second. Therefore, biochemical research workers do their best to identify and enhance every metabolic factor that can affect sports ability.

Nutritional Means

Energy is required for physical exercise, so naturally people are highly interested in energy metabolism. As early as 1958, researchers at the Beijing College of Physical Education found that blood glucose levels of marathon runners decreased significantly during a race. In 1975, the Institute of Sports Medicine of the Beijing Medical College showed that a sugar supplement of 1 to 2 g/kg of body weight would maintain the blood glucose levels of exercising athletes. The same conclusions were obtained by Chen Jidi and colleagues in human experiments and by Fang Yu and colleagues in animal experiments.

For the purpose of determining protein requirements, nitrogen balance as well as hemoglobin, serum protein, and urine creatinine levels were examined in children and in gymnasts, weight lifters, footballers (soccer players), and volleyball players, with nitrogen balance as the major criterion. The authors inferred that the protein requirement of athletes was higher than that of ordinary people.

A number of studies on water and electrolyte metabolism were conducted. Information on perspiration rate and the mineral and trace element contents in sweat were obtained. This information has provided the theoretical basis for research on athletes' requirements for water and electrolytes and made possible the correct manufacture of sports drinks. Since 1984, increased attention has been given to studies on trace elements. Atomic absorption spectrophotometry and neutron activation methods were used to analyze iron, magnesium, copper, zinc, manganese, cobalt, chromium, selenium, bromine, and iodine in the hair and the serum of athletes. These studies probed to a certain degree trace element requirements, changes of trace element concentrations in serum and tissues during physical exercise, and the relationship between their levels and athletic capacity.

As early as 1962, Chen Jidi and colleagues studied gymnasts and middle- and long-distance runners to determine their vitamin C requirements. It was found that physical exercise raised both vitamin C metabolism and requirements.

Wide interest and much importance has recently been attached to sports drinks as nutritional supplements. There were no Chinese sports drinks in the early 1980s, but now there are a Kiwi sport drink, "Jianlibao" sport drink, and fructus hippophae sport drink. Chinese investigators believe these drinks can truly enhance sports performance; in the 1984 Olympic Games they were nicknamed "magic drinks."

Pharmacological Techniques

Recent research has shown that traditional Chinese medicinal tonics can enhance sports performance. Since 1980 there have been more than 20 papers on this subject. Some tonics contain a single herb such as *Acanthoparax senticosus*, *Panax pseudoginseng*, *astiagalus membranaceous*, ginseng, pallen,

Traditional Chinese medicinal treatments are employed to speed recovery from sports injuries.

and *Ji's radix et rhizoma rhcdiolae*. There are also pellets, syrups, and instant drinks made from complex prescriptions. Human and animal experiments have shown that these tonics are good to a certain degree for regulating metabolism, aiding in recovery from fatigue, and elevating sports performance.

Biochemical Evaluation of Functional Status

In recent years, biochemical studies have examined the changes in metabolism and intermediary substances during physical exercise. The objective was to determine criteria that reflect fatigue and could be used to assess the functional status of athletes. Some of these studies have yielded positive preliminary results.

Endocrine Metabolism and Sports

Chinese studies on hormonal metabolism have included the analysis of plasma (or serum) testosterone, estradiol, thyrotropic hormone, thyroxine T_3 and T_4, cortisol, aldosterone, urinary luteinizing hormone, 17-hydroxysteroids, and

Talent, dedication, and research lead to ultimate success.

17-ketosteroids. Preliminary studies on athletes have shown that (1) the serum testosterone levels of elite Chinese sportswomen are lower than those of the ordinary people (tall women athletes exceeding 2 meters in height have even lower levels) before periods of competition; (2) serum testosterone levels rose nearly 100 percent after anaerobic physical exercise for 30 seconds but decreased in the recovery phase after long periods of physical exercise and could not be completely recovered even 24 hours afterwards; (3) the luteinizing hormone in the urine of exercising athletes decreased (the heavier the exercise, the lower the content); and (4) when exhausted after 80 percent $\dot{V}O_2$max exercise, the plasma levels of estradiol, aldosterone, and thyrotropic hormone of sportswomen increased significantly, while those of male sportsmen showed no changes.

Enzyme Metabolism and Sports

Yang Zeyi has published more than 10 papers on sports and enzymes during the last 5 to 6 years. These papers examined lactic acid dehydrogenase (LDH) and its isoenzymes, phosphocreatine kinase (CPK), and ATPase of red cells. Yang found that as criteria for evaluating a person's functional status, enzyme metabolic changes are very sensitive and highly specific. Isoenzymes in particular can reflect the metabolic status of different tissues and organs such as skeletal muscle, cardiac muscle, and the liver.

Metabolites and Mediators

Many investigators have conducted research on the metabolites and mediators such as catecholamine, lactic acid, enkephalins, r-aminobutyric acid, and hydroproline. Some significant results were obtained. For instance, very high or very low urinary excretion of catecholamine were found to often indicate poor function, and an increase in r-aminobutyric acid was found to be related to the central inhibition after fatigue caused by physical exercise. All types of physical exercise were observed to cause an elevation in the urinary excretion of hydroxyproline.

Immunity Function and Serum Protein

Some investigators have assessed the functional status of athletes by their immunity function and constituents of serum protein. It was found that (1) nonadaptation at the early stage of heavy training might cause significant decreases in serum immunoprotein IgG and IgA; (2) cellular and humoral immunity both significantly decreased after more than 15 minutes of running and could not be completely recovered even after 2.5 hours; and (3) when the functional status of an athlete became worse, the ratio of his serum γ (gamma) and α_2 (alpha-2) globulin was decreased significantly.

Biochemical Studies on Special Problems in Sports

Biochemical studies have also examined special problems in sports in an attempt to obtain practical information for athletes. Weight reduction, weight control, and drug control are research areas recently receiving emphasis.

Weight Reduction and Control

Certain competitive sports, such as weight lifting, judo, and wrestling, are divided into various body weight classes. Success in certain other sports (such as gymnastics, diving, and acrobatics) is closely related to body weight. The problem of maintenance of appropriate body weight becomes critical to those athletes.

Chinese investigators have considered this problem and began studies in 1979. Chen Jidi found that weight reduction could cause problems in protein, electrolytes, vitamins, fluid balance, as well as acid-base balance. Such problems can be determintal to the athletic ability and health of athletes. Research projects have sought to counteract these metabolic disturbances by introducing fortified food, and some good results have been obtained. In human and animal experiments conducted by Yan Zeyi and colleagues on water and electrolyte metabolism during rapid reductions in body weight, disturbances in water and electrolyte metabolism were corrected to a certain extent by supplementation of the diet with pills of an inorganic salt mixture.

Weight restriction in women gymnasts is a difficult problem that has not yet been solved. However, in recent years, prolonged observations of the metabolism of various nutritional factors and body composition were performed on women gymnasts undergoing weight control programs, and the results obtained provided a basis for taking practical steps with individual athletes as well as adding to the theoretical knowledge in this field.

Doping (or Drug) Control

International doping control and testing started in the late 1960s. In preparation for the 1990 Asian Games in Beijing, work in this area was recently accelerated. Determinations of some of the anabolic steriods can now be performed. At the same time, preliminary studies on whether some of the Chinese medicines contain banned drugs have also begun.

Outlook for Sports Physiology and Sports Biochemistry

Although work in sports physiology and sports biochemistry started rather late in China, the progress of these two branches has been rapid during the past ten years because of the advancement of science and technology as a whole and the application of new laboratory methods. The future prospects of these two branches are excellent.

The focus of research has been progressing from organs and the body as a whole to the cellular and subcellular levels. For example, the effects of physical exercise on the mitochondria and other microstructures, the effect of physical exercise on electrolyte constituents and fluid distribution, and the metabolism and dynamics of energy substances at the cellular level during physical exercise are being studied.

Through physiological and biochemical studies on subjects such as $\dot{V}O_2$max, anaerobic threshold, heart physiology after physical training, the relationship between fast and slow muscle fibers, and the metabolism of energy source substances, water, electrolytes, trace elements, and hormones, researchers hope to find the means for improving the scientific training of athletes, including nutritional aspects and methods of recovery. Sensitive and systematic physiological and biochemical means will be employed to assess the functional condition of athletes and to direct the training and selection of candidates scientifically. It is the present goal of Chinese sports science to develop and/or import increasingly sophisticated equipment and master techniques to strengthen the overall research effort.

Summary

Chinese scientists have made rapid progress since the end of the Cultural Revolution, bringing sports physiology and sports biochemistry into the mainstream of international research. Using modern techniques and aided by a new wave of young researchers, Chinese scientists are now interacting with their foreign colleagues through publications and international meetings. The refocused attention on conditioning, sports performance, and injury rehabilitation has aided Chinese athletes to compete at the highest levels of international competition.

Photo on facing page: Even simple exercise activities performed by elementary school children challenge the analyses of sports biomechanists.

Chapter 12

Sports Biomechanics—
Growth and Challenges
HUANG Zongcheng

Only 30 years have passed since the introduction of sports biomechanics to China. With the establishment of the China Sports Science Society in 1980 came increased advancement in the sports biomechanics field. Despite recent advances, Chinese scientists still face many challenges in sports biomechanics research.

Development of Sports Biomechanics

Like most sports sciences, sports biomechanics research began later in China than in other nations and had to overcome several barriers. Recently, the state

183

has increased its attention to sports biomechanics, and the number of personnel and amount of academic exchange in this field has grown.

Sports Biomechanics Established

The study of the modern science of sports biomechanics in China began in 1958 (shortly after the creation of biomechanics internationally) and gained initial development during the years leading up to 1980. During this period there was a lack of specialized personnel, information, and equipment. In 1980, there were only some 30 persons engaged in teaching or scientific research in this field, and sports biomechanics was taught only as an optional course and in only a few physical culture institutes. Due to the lack of teachers and laboratory equipment, teaching quality was then very poor. Before 1980 China had only one research group engaged in sports biomechanical studies (at the National Research Institute of Sports Science) and only a few persons specializing in this field at other research institutes.

Using hand-operated stopwatches and tapes, researchers carried out studies on the athletic field. Collecting large amounts of data, they analyzed the biomechanical features of certain sports events and made technical diagnoses for improving the performances of elite athletes.

For instance, Lü Qiang studied sprinting techniques using stopwatches to record split times and tapes to record stride lengths. The investigators arrived at the following conclusions: (1) Chinese sprinters took four or five more strides to complete the 100-meter run than did their foreign counterparts; (2) the markedly decreased speed of the Chinese runners toward the end of the race was due to a shortening of their strides and particularly a decrease in stride frequency; (3) the Chinese runners' shorter strides resulted primarily from poor running technique, although the shorter length of their legs was also a factor. These findings helped the Chinese sprinters change their technique and improve their performances. Researchers in other events also yielded positive results, which in turn stimulated the interest of coaches and athletes in the study of sports biomechanics and promoted the growth of this branch of learning.

Increasing Attention to Sports Biomechanics

With the state attaching greater importance to the advancement of science and education and with the steady development of sports and physical education, the need for raising athletic standards by scientific means was more and more strongly felt and greater attention was paid to the study of sports biomechanics. Consequently, the China Sports Science Society was established in 1980, and the Sports Biomechanics Society was formed under it. The establishment of the Sports Biomechanics Society marked a new stage in the development of this branch of learning.

With the Sports Biomechanics Society as the nucleus, all the specialists in various universities and research institutes were organized and united. In the years since then, much has been done to promote academic exchanges at home and with other countries. As an organization affiliated with the China Sports Science Society, the Sports Biomechanics Society became a member of both the International Biomechanics Society and the International Sports Biomechanics Society in 1985. By 1986, the membership of the Society had grown to over 280. Thanks to the Society's efforts and the support given it by the various departments concerned, great progress has been achieved over the past few years.

Also in 1980, by decision of the State Physical Education and Sports Commission and the State Education Commission, sports biomechanics was made an obligatory course at all physical culture institutes and in physical education departments at all institutes of higher learning. Sports biomechanical laboratories were established at certain physical education institutes and in physical education departments of certain universities. These laboratories were supplied with advanced equipment for teaching and research. The physical culture institutes in Beijing, Shanghai, Tianjin, and Chengdu boast such modern devices as 3-dimensional (3-D) force platforms and high-speed cameras.

Personnel and Institutes

To meet the growing needs in biomechanical teaching and research, specialized personnel have been drawn from the fields of physics, mechanics, biology, and sports. Such persons have gone through short-term courses or have studied sports biomechanics through their own efforts. Since 1982, China has produced some 20 graduates and postgraduates in this field. At present, there are seven institutions in the country that have admitted postgraduate students completing study for the master's degree in sports biomechanics. This academic title is also obtainable from the National Research Institute of Sports Science in Beijing.

Increased attention has been paid to sports biomechanics by sports research institutes all over the country. Research groups with specialized personnel of various technical status have been formed at institutes in such places as Beijing, Shanghai, and Jiangsu. The National Research Institute of Sports Science, for instance, has a sports biomechanics laboratory that is equipped with an IPL synchronous high-speed camera, 3-D force platforms of different types, a Selspot II system, a film analysis system, and a film and video analysis system. The Jiangsu Sports Research Institute has purchased whole sets of equipment for the study of sports biomechanics. The sports research institutes in some provinces and cities have made sports biomechanics key items in their research programs for the near future.

During recent years, electronic equipment has been acquired to aid biomechanics research.

In its long-term plan for scientific and technical development for the remaining years of this century, the State Physical Education and Sports Commission has listed sports biomechanics alongside exercise physiology, sports biochemistry, and sport psychology as a key subject to be studied.

Academic Exchange

A dozen or so well known scholars and experts in sports biomechanics have been invited to come to China to give lectures and provide consultation. Their visits have helped promote sports biomechanical studies in this country. Meanwhile, China has sent representatives to other countries on study tours or to take part in international academic meetings at which Chinese papers were presented. China has also sent a number of scholars to the United States, the Federal Republic of Germany, and Japan for advanced studies.

Domestically, 10 national academic meetings were held during the period from 1980 to 1986. These included five national seminars between 1980 and 1985—one for studying teaching methods in 1983, two for discussing research methods in 1984 and 1985, one for studying video analyses, and another for reviewing the trends in the development of sports biomechanics in 1986. Altogether, 707 persons attended these meetings and 431 papers were presented. Regional academic meetings were also held in the eastern, northern, south-central, and northeastern sections of China, with a total of 180 participants presenting 83 papers. Conferences were also held at the provincial and municipal levels to discuss individual topics. All these activities have helped to disseminate the fruits of research, stimulate the exchange of experiences, spread information and academic viewpoints, and speed development of young personnel with potential for research and teaching.

Challenges for Today and the Future

In spite of the rapid progress made in recent years, China still lags far behind the world's leaders in sports biomechanics. Under the impact of the world technical revolution, sports in the coming years will develop on a broader scale and sports standards will be improved at a faster rate than ever before. More attention will be given to improving athletic training and upgrading athletic performances by scientific means. This trend manifests itself most clearly in countries that are more advanced in science and technology. In a certain sense, international sports contests in the future will be contests in scientific progress. Sports biomechanics will be one of the most important instruments by which these contests are waged. To meet the needs of sports development at home and to catch up with the world's best in this branch of study, China must concentrate on the following tasks as identified by the Commission on Research Policy.

Attracting More Qualified Personnel

A major factor accounting for the backward state of sports biomechanics in China is the shortage of specialized personnel in this field, both numerically and in terms of quality. At present, China has only 30 or so research workers specializing in sports biomechanics and some 100 teachers, only about 20 of whom have gone through systematic specialized training at college or postgraduate levels. Every year, only a dozen or so students of sports biomechanics finish their college or postgraduate courses. This number falls far short of what is needed.

At a conference on the strategy in sports biomechanics development held in Suzhou in 1986, it was envisaged that, by 1990, China would need some 100 teachers and researchers in this field, more than double the number that can be expected if the present rate of growth is maintained. To fill this gap, measures must be taken to increase the enrollment of students in colleges and postgraduate studies. Young people demonstrating great potential should be sent abroad for advanced studies, while refresher courses should be given to those on the job. Only through diversified needs can a large number of qualified personnel of various grades be produced.

Increasing the Number of Research Facilities and the Standard of Research

Since sports performances are highly complicated, it is very difficult to reveal the biomechanical laws governing the movements of the human body in sports training and competition unless we are armed with different kinds of practical yet highly sophisticated instruments. In China, many research institutes have purchased modern equipment from abroad and also have at their disposal domestically produced equipment such as 3-D force platforms, film analysis systems, and 8-channel telemetering electromyographs. However, existing equipment remains far from adequate for teaching and research, and must be improved or replaced.

Emphasizing the Use of Computers

The development of a new branch of learning depends much on the development of research methods. Therefore, from 1980 to 1986 four special meetings were held to discuss research methods being used inside and outside China and to draw up unified objectives and requirements to be fulfilled in future research. The concensus opinion was that the key to building better sports biomechanics laboratories and improving research methods lay in computerization. The use of computers is a hallmark of the progress of world science in the 1980s. Computers not only greatly enhance work efficiency and precision in calculations, but are capable of producing vast amounts of data in experiments. Sports biomechanics researchers in many countries have used computers for the whole spectrum of their work— testing, simulating, preparing statistics, calculating, producing graphs, and tabulating results. With a computer, immediate results can be obtained by recording kinematical and kinetical indexes simultaneously. The data thus obtained can provide valuable feedback for athletic practice.

With computers the study of sports biomechanics has entered a new stage. Researchers in the United States have achieved remarkable results by using computers to study the techniques and tactics of certain sports. Some scholars maintain that the use of computers has set off a revolution in sports competition and that the computer can play a vital role in determining the outcome of a sports contest. In China, there is a growing awareness of the importance of computers in scientific research. At the Fourth National Sports Biomechanics Symposium in 1983, some scholars presented papers describing how computers were used to simulate sports techniques and to smooth data. Presently, many laboratories and scientific research units use computers for video tests and analyses and for automatic and immediate treatment of data. The use of computers in sports biomechanics research will help shorten the time required for the compilation of research projects, speed up the process of feedback, increase social benefits, and accelerate the overall progress of sports biomechanics.

Studying Both the Practical Application and Basic Theories of Sports Biomechanics

Experience in other countries shows the importance of sports biomechanics as an applied science. Developments in China over the last few years have also demonstrated the vitality of sports biomechanics in helping to escalate the quality of sports performance and the need to combine research with practical application.

Thirty-seven papers, or 36.2 percent of the total presented at the Fourth Sports Biomechanics Symposium in 1984, dealt with the question of how technical investigations had led to improvement of sports performances. These included a technical analysis of high-jumper Zhu Jianhua's world record performance (2.38 meters) and another one on weight lifter Wu Shude's world-record snatching performance (128 kg). These studies were of practical significance in popularizing advanced techniques as well as promoting the progress of sports biomechanics. A number of sports biomechanics research items were commended by the State Sports Commission in 1985 for their excellent results. These included the following:

- A sports biomechanical analysis of the techniques of Zhu Jianhua, world record setter in the men's high jump
- A study on the resistance factors in cycling; experiments on the rider and his bike in a wind tunnel
- A study of the giant swing on the gymnastic rings
- A study of stable landings off the vaulting horse
- A report on the diagnosis of sprinting techniques
- A study on shooting technique in the standing position
- A biomechanical analysis of pole-vaulting techniques
- The manufacture and assembly of the ST-85 type 16mm film analysis system
- The manufacture of a sports techniques film analysis system

All of these studies dealt with problems demanding immediate solution and were of great practical significance.

The study of basic theories constitutes the foundation for the development of sports biomechanics as a new branch of learning. A weak foundation will, in the long run, adversely affect the progress of the science and reduce its practical value. Attention must be paid to the study of the basic movements of the human body and the basic parameters related to them so that researchers can identify basic laws governing these movements and the mechanism by which they are generated. Too little has been done in this respect, and efforts are now being made by some universities of science and engineering to fill the gap.

Advancing Sports Biomechanics
While Fulfilling Practical Assignments

Experience has shown that sports biomechanics is capable of helping to improve sports performances. In recent years, the performance level of sports in many countries has risen almost simultaneously with the development of sports biomechanics. Many training centers for ranking athletes have complete biomechanics laboratories.

It is an important task for sports biomechanics researchers to serve the needs of athletic training. Many research projects in China are undertaken by research workers in cooperation with coaches and athletes. Studies are made right on the athletic field, with athletic performances filmed and analysed to provide data for technical improvement. Consider the men's high jump, for example. Biomechanical studies of such aspects as the approach run, the takeoff, and movements over the bar proved helpful to high-jumpers Ni Zhiqin and Zhu Jianhua in their efforts to establish world records. In gymnastics, Ma Yanhong succeeded in incorporating a Japanese dismount off the horizontal bar into her back roll straddle dismount off the uneven bars to earn a perfect score of 10 points at the 23rd World Gymnastics Championships. She owed much of her success to the help of a quantitative analysis of a simulated exercise. In cycling, experiments in a wind tunnel were carried out with the riders form-

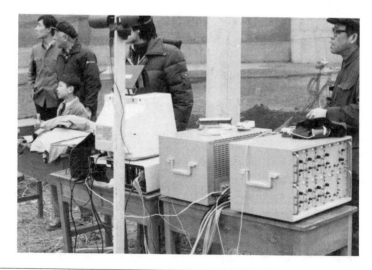

Biomechanists use telemetering and electronic instruments to study athletes at the site of an outdoor competition.

ing a file to determine how far apart they should be spaced to reduce wind resistance to the minimum. In volleyball, a study on spiking techniques revealed that the optimal height for Lang Ping's spikes was 2.87 meters.

Expanding Research Work

With the improvement of research methods, the acquisition of equipment, and the elevation of expertise, China's research productivity will develop in the following ways: (1) It will include quantitative as well as qualitative analyses. (2) Studies will involve multiple indices rather than a single index. (3) Technical analyses of sports involving individual efforts will be replaced by overall tactical and technical analyses of sports involving team efforts.

China today boasts a 300-strong contingent of workers in the field of sports biomechanics, including scientists and specialists at sports research institutes, teachers at physical education colleges or departments, and sports enthusiasts at large. Their scientific studies cover a wide range of subjects, including technical diagnoses for sports performances, mathematical modeling and computer simulation, studies on body segment parameters, and studies on research

Mu Xiangxiong, China's first world record breaker in swimming, heralded the rapid advancement in swimming aided by sports science research.

methodology, with considerable achievements every year. At the Fifth National Sports Biomechanics Symposium in 1985, for instance, 153 papers were submitted and 78 were read during the sessions, including 33 (or 42.8%) on sports techniques, 22 (27.3%) on applied or theoretical studies, and 18 (23.4%) on the study of apparatuses or application of computers.

Progressively higher precision will be achieved in future research. In studying high-level techniques in competitive sports, precise data and intrinsic laws can hardly be obtained by qualitative analyses or theoretical deduction. Investigations have now advanced to a higher stage, which is characterized by on-the-spot experiments and tests and quantitative analyses of sports techniques by means of highly precise instruments. In this way, various mechanical parameters in relation to human movements are accurately determined. Thus the Selspot II system and the 3-D force platform are simultaneously employed to detect the three-dimensional wobbling movements of an elite shooter while taking aim in the standing position, as well as the movement of the combined center of gravity of both shooter and weapon. With a computer, various data and graphs can be promptly obtained. High-speed cameras can be used to show the slightest changes in movement. With a 3-D force platform and film analyses, we can detect the changes of force in an exercise. By applying these methods, gratifying results have also been achieved in studying techniques in such areas as track-and-field, swimming, and gymnastics.

Summary

The development of sports biomechanics in China over the last two or three decades has proved that sports performances can be improved with the help of up-to-date scientific means. With the advancement of world science, sports biomechanics will be further enriched by modern scientific theories and methods and make faster progress than ever. With the support of the government and other quarters, the sports biomechanics workers in China will continue their efforts to meet the growing needs of sports development. In the light of the Chinese athletes' body shapes, functions, and qualities, they will strive to find ways of improving technical performances that will suit them best. It is hoped that by the end of this century, China will catch up with the rest of the world in the field of sports biomechanics.

Photo on facing page: Psychological and physiological mechanisms interact in taijiquan.

Chapter 13

Development of Sport Psychology

MA Qiwei

The Chinese people have a relatively long history of interest in sport psychology, although the history of scientific investigation is relatively short. Most recently, a surge of interest following the end of the Cultural Revolution in 1976 resulted in rapid development of research and national societies for the exchange of information and advancement of knowledge.

Development of Sport Psychology in Ancient and Modern China

Much rich psychological thought is contained in China's cultural heritage, which has a history of over 3,000 years dating from the time before the Qin Dynasty (221-206 B.C.). But only a hundred years ago did Chinese scholars first become aware of Western psychology. It was not until the new school system and modern Western science were introduced into China early this century that psychology in China became an independent discipline.

In the Qing Dynasty (A.D. 1644-1911), psychology was offered as a course first at Tongwen School and the Normal School, and later at some intermediate normal schools. After the Revolution of 1911, psychology was offered at institutions of higher learning. In 1917, China's first laboratory of psychology was set up in Beijing University. Around 1920, psychologists of the older generation (e.g., Chen Daqi, Tang Jin, and Lu Zhiwei) returned from studies abroad to lead the modern development of psychology in China. In 1920, the first department of psychology was set up at South East University.

In 1921, the China Society of Psychology was established. In 1928, the Research Institute of Psychology was set up, followed in 1931 by the China Society of Psychological Testing, the China Society of Psychohygiene, and the China Society of Psychoanalysis. During this period, departments of psychology were set up at more than 10 universities, including the Central University, Qinghua University, Fudan University, the Catholic University, and Daxia University.

Before 1937, psychology, educational psychology, child psychology, and psychohygiene were taught in departments of pedagogy and physical education in institutions of higher education, but sport psychology was not offered. In 1933, the Physical Education Department of Beijing Normal University, which was the earliest department of its kind in the country, began offering such courses as physical education theory, biomechanics of sports, and biochemistry and exercise physiology, but sport psychology was not offered.

Interest in sport psychology began to surface during this period, however. A substantial number of articles were written on the relationship between physical education and psychology. A significant article is the "Study of Physical Education," written by the late Chairman Mao Zedong in his early years. He pointed out that "physical education strengthens the bones and the muscles of the body. . . . It can also increase knowledge . . . adjust feelings . . . and cultivate willpower."

Another significant article, titled "Transfer Value of Physical Education" and published in 1926 by Ma Yuehan (John Ma), a veteran professor in physical education, regarded sports as "a very good place to foster the students' character and morals. There, mistakes can be criticized, nobility encouraged, temperament moulded, and good qualities inspired." He held that "a young man's courage, strong willpower, self-confidence, enterprising spirit, and determination to win can be cultivated'' through hard training. Moreover, he pointed out, ''The character and morals exhibited on the sports ground can be transferred'' and would affect a person throughout life. In short, the seed of sport psychology had been growing in the fields of physical education and psychology before 1937 (the year of the Japanese military invasion), despite the fact that sport psychology was not offered as a physical education course at institutions of higher learning at that time.

This statue is dedicated to professor Ma Yuehan (John Ma), a pioneer in Chinese physical education.

In 1942, Wu Wenzhong and Xiao Zhongguo, faculty members of the then National Institute of Wushu and Physical Education, edited *Psychology on Physical Education*, which was the first book in China to deal with physical education and sport psychology. The book has five chapters, all translated from other sources, entitled ''General Discussion,'' ''Ideal Physical Education,'' ''Discovery of Physical Education and Sports,'' ''Sports Analysis,'' and ''Influence of Sports.''

Development of Sport Psychology in the New China

The People's Republic of China was founded in 1949. Under the leadership of the Chinese Communist Party and the People's Government, socialist economic construction, culture, education, and science have increasingly developed. These changes have provided an environment for the rapid development of psychology in China.

During the period from 1949 to 1956, the necessary organizational structure and personnel was basically completed and the long-term program for the development of psychology formulated. In 1950, preparations began for the establishment of the Chinese Academy of Sciences. During the nationwide adjustments of universities and their departments in 1952, departments of psychology from Qinghua University and Yanjing University were merged into the Department of Philosophy at Beijing University. However, at Nanjing University, the Department of Psychology remained intact. Faculty members in other psychology departments were assigned to teaching and research groups at teachers' colleges, medical academies, and physical education institutions in various parts of the country. As part of the national program for the development of sciences, a 12-year program of development for psychology was formulated in 1956; it subsequently became one of the basic disciplines. In the same year, the Research Institute of Psychology was set up. The major publications during this period were *Journal of Psychology*, *Newsletter of Psychology*, and *Translation on Psychology*, all edited by the Society of Psychology.

In order to learn psychology from the Soviet Union, the Central Ministry of Education invited Soviet psychologists to lecture in China between 1952 and 1956. The study and discussion of Pavlov's theory was a primary topic in the academic circles of psychology, medicine, and physiology, leading to some exploratory research projects. At that time, only a few lectures on sport psychology were given by foreign scholars. In 1957 *Psychology*, written by Soviet scholar P.A. Rudik and translated by Sun Jinghao, became available in China. The book contained considerable information about physical education and served as a major reference book for sport psychologists in China. *Questions on Sport Psychology*, written by Chernikewa of the Soviet Union and translated by Wang Bing in 1958, became the main reference in the teaching of sport psychology at physical education institutions.

During the 10 years (1956-1966) of socialist construction, psychologists in China took Marxism as a guiding principle in an attempt to develop an approach to psychology that would be suitable for serving the socialist economy and culture. At the same time, they tried to regulate and fulfill the long-term plan developed in 1956. The teachers and researchers of this period completed many studies on fundamental psychological processes, psychophysiological functions, and developmental psychology. Through the joint development of physical education and psychology, and with the introduction of sport psychology resources from abroad, more sport psychology resources were compiled and translated by the physical education institutions of Beijing, Wuhan, and Shanghai. Toward the end of the 1950s and in the early 1960s, sport psychology gradually became a formal course offered at all institutions of physical education.

Just as this golden opportunity for the development of the science emerged, a leftist ideological trend launched a nationwide campaign to criticize the so-called bourgeois orientation of psychology. The "biologicalization" and "abstraction" in psychology were harshly and wrongly criticized. In response, psychologists in 1959 conducted discussions of the basic issues—namely, the object, method, and task of psychology and its nature, in accordance with the policy put forth by Mao Zedung of "letting a hundred flowers blossom and a hundred schools of thought contend." The academic atmosphere was very lively throughout these discussions. In 1960, the congress of the Society of Psychology summed up the result of these discussions and formulated a 3-year research program. Later, a commission of educational psychology was set up and a 5-year program on the study of children's psychological age characteristics was worked out, thus promoting the development of teaching and scientific research.

Then, during the Cultural Revolution from 1966 to 1976, the ultraleft trend of thought again invaded psychology. Yao Wenyuan (using Ge Ming as an assumed name), a literary ruffian, wrote in a Shanghai newspaper article in October 1965 labeling psychology a bourgeois pseudoscience. This precipitated 10 chaotic years and a continuation of the erroneous criticism that started in 1958. During this time many psychologists were attacked for their ideas; some were labeled as "reactionary academic authority," and others were even put to death. Teaching and research organizations were forced to close and

The joy of effort—a psychological reward.

their staffs dispersed. Naturally, the emerging field of sport psychology also suffered destruction in this political storm.

With the smashing of the "Gang of Four" in October 1976 came a scientific renaissance. The Research Institute of Psychology was restored in June 1977, and in August of that year a forum for discussing the long-term development of psychology was convened in Pinggu County of Beijing. The results included another readjustment of the long-term direction of psychology and the restoration of teaching and research organizations. Departments of psychology were set up in Beijing University, Hangzhou University, East China Normal University, and Beijing Normal University. In order to meet the needs of China's four modernizations, beginning in 1978 seven specialized commissions were established by the China Society of Psychology. They are

- the Developmental Psychology and Educational Commission;
- the Basic Psychology Theory Commission;
- the Medical Psychology Commission;
- the Physical Education and Sport Psychology Commission;
- the General Psychology and Experimental Psychology Commission;
- the Industrial Psychology Commission; and
- the Physiological Psychology Commission.

Establishment of the China Society of Sport Psychology

In May 1978, a symposium on developmental and educational psychology was organized in Hangzhou by the China Society of Psychology. During the meeting, scholars interested in sport psychology exchanged views and suggested the idea of establishing a specialized commission. In December 1978, at the Second Annual Academic Meeting of the China Society of Psychology held in Baoding, Hebei province, a preparatory group responsible for the establishment of a specialized commission was organized with the approval of the Council of the China Society of Psychology. In November 1979, at the Third Annual Academic Meeting of the China Society of Psychology held in Tianjin, the Physical Education and Sport Psychology Commission was officially established.

More than 30 sport psychologists took part in this annual meeting. Out of the 22 papers submitted by them, 10 were read and discussed at the meeting, including

- "A Survey of Sport Psychology Abroad";
- "Psychological Factors of Self-Training Process in Volleyball Game";
- "Sense Signal in Physical Education Teaching and Training";

- ''Psychological Training and Self-Control'';
- ''Examination of Character Classification and Its Relation With Sports Events and Athletes''; and
- ''Application of Relaxation Response to the Training, Competition, Recovery After Competition, Eliminating Morbid State of Athletes.''

This was the first time sport psychologists had an organized academic program since the founding of New China. Ma Qiwei, Liu Shennian, and five other persons were elected unanimously as committee members. Zhao Bin, vice-director, and Que Yongwu, secretary-general, both from the preparatory committee responsible for setting up the China Sports Science Society, paid a special visit to the meeting and gave a brief introduction of their preparatory work.

In December 1980, the inaugural meeting of the China Sports Science Society was held in Beijing. During the meeting, a Society of Sport Psychology within the China Sports Science Society was established. The first committee of the Society, composed of 11 members, was formed through consultation and election. Among the eleven members, Ma Qiwei, Xu Lianlun, Wu Youyin, Liu Shennian, and Qiu Yijun were members of the standing committee responsible for leadership, with Ma Qiwei as president, Xu Lianlun as vice-president, and Wu Youyin as secretary-general. The two organizations, the Society of Sport Psychology and the Physical Education and Sport Psychology Commission, have the same membership and are under the dual leadership of the China Sports Science Society and China Society of Psychology. Later, the Society of Sport Psychology and the Physical Education and Sport Psychology Commission were set up at provincial levels throughout the country. Up to the present, there are about 20 academic organizations of sport psychology throughout the country.

In September 1984, the Second Congress of the China Sports Science Society was held and the leading bodies of the general Society and its subordinate societies of various specialties were reelected. The second committee of the Society of Sport Psychology is composed of 23 members, 8 of whom are members of the standing committee. They are Ma Qiwei, president (professor at Beijing Institute of Physical Education); Xu Lianlun, vice-president (director at the Research Institute of Psychology under the Chinese Academy of Sciences); Liu Shennian, vice-president (professor at Harbin Normal University); Ding Xueqian, deputy secretary-general; Chen Shuyong (professor at Beijing University); Xie Sancai (professor at Shenyang Institute of Physical Education); Cao Qigang (associate professor at Hebei Normal University); and Qiu Yijun (associate professor at Wuhan Institute of Physical Education). The Society now has a membership of about 200.

Although sport psychology is in its infancy in China, with each passing day this emerging discipline is developing.

Scientific Research

The early 1960s saw a blossoming of scientific research in sport psychology. Initial research was conducted on such topics as the object and contents of sport psychology, the motive of sports enthusiasts in sports participation, the effect of language instruction on sports performance, and the appearance of psychological barriers during competition. Lacking a unified research program, the topics studied were not centered on the more important topics in the field. It was not until the establishment of the preparatory group responsible for the formation of the Physical Education and Sport Psychology Commission in 1978 that psychologists, physical educators, and coaches began to conduct more systematic research in sport psychology. During the Third Annual Academic Meeting of the China Society of Psychology in 1979, 22 sport psychology papers were read at the symposium organized by the newly established Physical Education and Sport Psychology Commission. Results of research from abroad were also presented at the symposium. The research orientation was further developed through intense discussion of the papers. From this, a research program was formulated requiring the cooperation of psychologists, physical education workers, and sports coaches. This was a significant step toward a well-focused research program in sport psychology.

Symposia and Studies in Sport Psychology

Since the founding of the China Sports Science Society, eight national symposia have been held in a relatively short period. The first symposium was held in Tianjin in November 1979. The Physical Education and Sport Psychology Commission was established at this meeting. The second symposium was held in Beijing in December 1980, at which the Society of Sport Psychology under the China Sports Science Society was established. The third symposium was held in Beijing in December 1981 at an annual meeting of the China Society of Psychology. The fourth symposium, held in Kunming in August 1983, was sponsored by the Society of Sport Psychology. The fifth symposium was held in Chengdu in October 1985 and was cosponsored by the Society of Sport Psychology and the Society of Sports Training. This was the first time that this kind of joint conference has been organized. It was very successful and helpful both to the psychologists and the coaches. They began to share common ideas about scientific sport training.

The sixth symposium was held in Hangzhou in September 1987 during the 60th Anniversary Congress of the China Society of Psychology. The seventh symposium was held in Shijiazhong in December 1987 during the Third Congress of China Society of Sport Sciences. The eighth symposium was held in Penglei, Shandong province, in October 1989. It was decided on this occa-

Table 13.1   Categories of Sport Psychology Research Papers Presented in China Between 1979 and 1985

Category	Percentage (%)
Psychology related to specific sports events	21.06
Character, personality, and neurotypes	15.79
Psychological training	12.28
Theory of sport psychology	9.65
Teaching of physical education	8.77
Developing psychological ability	7.89
Psychology of competition	7.89
Methods of psychological testing	7.02
Social psychology of sport	5.26
Psychological selection of athletes	4.39

sion that a national symposium will be organized by the China Society of Sport Psychology every other year.

From all these symposia, more than 200 papers were presented. In Table 13.1 the subjects of these papers are categorized.

Many of the studies reported were conducted by psychologists collaborating with teachers of physical education and coaches of sport. The focus of the research was to integrate theory with teaching and training practice. Examples of these studies are as follows:

"The Effect of Training in Thinking on the Teaching of Hurdles."   A research paper completed by a psychology teacher of the Teachers' Physical Education College and a physical education teacher of China Political Science and Law University. Through the study both theoretical and practical knowledge about teaching methods were improved.

"Mental Rehearsal Training and Movement Control."   A research paper completed by a psychology teacher of Beijing University and a coach of shooting. Through the study, the training methods for shooting improved, and the athletes' stability of movement and self-control were increased.

"Psychological Preparation of Gymnasts in Learning New and Difficult Elements and the Initial Study of Its Teaching Method."   A research paper completed by a research worker of Tianjin Sports Science Research Institute, a coach of Tianjin Gymnastic Team, and a physical education teacher of the Physical Education Department, Tianjin Normal University. This study sought to integrate psychological training with sports training. Through the study, theoretical knowledge of training was increased and better training results were achieved.

"An Experimental Research of the Effect of Strengthening the Motion-Perception Control on Shooting in Basketball Game." A research paper jointly completed by a teacher of the Psychology Department and a teacher of the Physical Education Department, both from Shandong Normal University. This study improved teaching methods.

These results prove the value of a research orientation requiring psychologists to go deep into teaching and training realities and to closely cooperate with teachers of physical education, sports coaches, and scientific research workers. In doing so, theory is combined with practice. As a result, the practical ability of theoretical workers is increased and the theoretical level of practical workers is upgraded. The quality of teaching, training, and sports performance are also improved. One example is a research paper entitled "Psychological Training for a Woman Shooter of Clay Pigeon," completed by a psychology researcher in collaboration with a shooting coach. This study not only put forward a scientific and systematic training method, but also played an active role in improving sports performance. The shooter later set a world record.

Books on Sport Psychology

The development of teaching resources for sport psychology in physical education institutions and departments began in the early 1960s. The first publication, the two-volume *Reference Material for Teaching Sport Psychology*, was written by members of the Beijing Institute of Physical Education in February and May 1962. The Physical Education Institutes of Tianjin, Wuhan, and Shanghai worked together from 1963 to 1964 to publish *The Trial Edition of Sport Psychology Teaching Material for Physical Education Institutes*. Beginning in 1979 after the Cultural Revolution, sport psychology books were compiled regularly by physical education institutions such as Shenyang Institute of Physical Education, Wuhan Institute of Physical Education, and Chengdu Institute of Physical Education.

In 1980, the State Physical Education and Sports Commission organized two groups of psychology specialists from physical education institutions to examine and approve the draft of the textbook *Psychology*, which was subsequently published. This book was designed to be used by physical education institutions and departments. Later, textbooks and reference books such as *Sport Psychology* and *Physical Education Psychology* were compiled and published successively by physical education and normal institutions.

International Academic Exchange

Since the founding of the Society of Sport Psychology, a policy of strengthening international academic exchanges has been pursued. Comparatively speaking, sport psychology in China is a new, emerging discipline. Only through strengthening international exchanges can China speed the development of the discipline. This is being pursued by inviting foreign experts to come to China and by sending Chinese sport psychologists abroad to participate in academic conferences. In 1981, Professor Ma Qiwei went to Ottawa, Canada, to attend the Fifth Congress of the International Society of Sport Psychology. At the meeting, he presented a lecture outlining the development of sport psychology in China. From then on, the door between Chinese sport psychologists and sport psychologists around the world was open. In 1982, international academic exchanges began. In the past few years, scholars such as Dr. Terry Orlick from University of Ottawa, Canada, Professor Kazuome Osada from Nippon College of Physical Education, Japan, Professor Bryant Cratty from University of California, Los Angeles, United States, Professor Hermann Rieder from University of Heidelberg, Federal Republic of Germany, and Dr. Robert Singer of the United States (and president of the International Society of Sport Psychology) have visited. In 1986, the China Society of Sport Psychology was admitted into the International Society of Sport Psychology, which has further broadened the possibilities for international academic exchanges.

For years China has sent scholars abroad to visit other countries and young graduate students to study at leading universities. These students are now studying in Canada, Japan, Germany, and the United States. The advanced theory and scientific techniques they learn helps hasten the growth and application of the discipline. As sport psychology continues to grow in China it promises to make great contributions to physical education and sports and to the spiritual and material well-being of the Chinese socialist society.

Summary

Sport psychology just recently developed in China, but it has done so rather quickly. Sport psychology is not only offered as a course in academic institutes but is also generally accepted and recognized for its importance by society. Academic and applied research is progressing broadly, especially in the area of applied sport psychology with elite athletes. Studies have been conducted on the psychological characteristics of elite athletes, psychological training and performance of athletes, and psychological consultation and diagnosis. Academically, sport psychology in China tends to emphasize cognitive psychology and psychophysiology. Some of the departments of sport psychology in key institutes of physical education are building special laboratories in these areas of investigation.

The Future
of Sport in China

P
A
R
T

I
I
I

Having examined the history and present organization of sport and physical education in China in Part I, and having seen the recent but rapid development of sports research in the People's Republic in Part II, we turn to Part III for a glance at the future.

The Chinese have set high goals for success in the sports arena. Chapter 14 looks at these goals and the methods China will use to accomplish these goals. In addition, the author shows how improving economic strength may boost the country's strategic goal of becoming a great sports power.

Photo on facing page: Figure skating is one of the newest sports in China.

Chapter 14

Looking Forward to the 21st Century
LIANG Zengshou

Having reviewed and discussed the past and present developments of sports in China, one naturally looks to the future. What are the prospects for China's physical culture and sports?

At the beginning of the 1980s, Chinese sports authorities suggested that China should become a world sports power within the century. The broad masses of coaches, athletes, and other people in the sports circles are striving for the realization of this strategic objective.

"A world sports power" is a complex notion. It suggests a three-dimensional network with many facets and layers, including popular physique, physical education, mass physical culture, competitive sports, sports talent, sports science and technology, sports fields and facilities, and sportsmanship, all of which are interrelated and interdependent. However, public opinion in the world generally holds that sports skills are the most salient and important feature of a world sports power. A country that fails to place itself among the most successful nations at the Olympics is not acknowledged as a great sports power, even if it has a highly developed mass sports system and outstanding sports facilities.

In the light of such criteria, Chinese sports experts have forecast that by the end of the century, China's sports will develop into a complex state, as follows:

- It will rank between third and fifth overall at the Olympics.
- In terms of the overall level of sports science and techniques, it will come close to the present leaders.
- It will make considerable progress in the improvement of the physique of the younger generation, the popularization of mass sports, the improvement of the conditions and quality of physical cultural education, and the development of sports fields and facilities.

Level of Sports Skills

Judged by their performances in international competition in recent years, athletes of the Soviet Union, the United States, and the German Democratic Republic have established them as the three foremost sports nations in the world. The Federal Republic of Germany comes next. While Bulgaria, Romania, and Hungary are slightly ahead of China, Cuba, Poland, Italy, and Japan, these countries are all more or less on the same par. South Korea has been progressing rapidly in recent years. As a whole, China at the moment ranks from eighth to tenth place in the sports world. This is the starting point from which we proceed toward the year 2000.

Judging by the progress that has been made in competitive sports during the past 10 years, and provided no serious mistakes are made in the coming years, China can be expected to rank fifth or sixth overall at the 25th Olympics in 1992 and fifth or even fourth at the 27th Olympics in 2000. If her Olympic strategy is effectively carried out, it would not be totally impossible for China to surpass the Democratic German Republic or the United States to rank third. In fact, China's sports circles are striving for this goal with full confidence.

Level of Sports Science and Technique

Proceeding from her financial strength and present level of sports development, China will make efforts to improve the training of her athletes in a systematic way by applying advanced science and techniques. China will concentrate its use of advanced training methods in only some of the events (one-third of them, for instance). This is important to ensure that China's sports level catches up with world standards.

To accommodate the 11th Asian Games and other major international sports competitions, including the Olympics if possible, China plans to equip stadiums and gymnasiums in a number of big cities with advanced technology, bringing them up to world standards. At present, the equipment of most of the stadiums and gymnasiums in the country is below the 1980s standard of the developed countries.

In sports science, China is expected to make break-throughs in some major disciplines and attain a number of internationally significant results to contribute to world sports science. She will be able to do so by intensively applying to training athletes and athletic injuries traditional Chinese therapies such as bone setting, massage, acupuncture, herbal medicine, qigong (breathing exercises), and martial arts. In the research of philosophy and other social sciences related to sports, China figures to be among the foremost nations in the world.

Other Aspects of Physical Culture

China will be much more developed than she is now in many aspects of physical culture. More and more people will take part in sports. As a form of culture,

Mass participation in exercise and sport as well as international success in the competitive arena are goals of the future.

sports will be closely linked with recreation, tourism, and health maintenance and will be integrated with them in some cases to become an important means of meeting the increasing cultural needs of the people. Cultural recreation centers will be built in urban neighborhoods and rural townships.

Throughout the country, there will be many training centers and sports fields with modern facilities. In those provincial and autonomous regional capital cities where conditions are conducive, sports facilities will be built that can meet the needs of major international competitions. In Beijing and Shanghai, sports centers meeting the highest world standards will be constructed. Physical culture education will be conducted in a systematic and scientific way, with comprehensive, systematic teaching systems and after-class training and competing systems instituted or perfected. Talented athletes will come forth in great numbers.

Economy and Sport

Due to historical and social reasons and her limited economic strength, it is unrealistic to expect China to reach the level of the world's athletic leaders by the year 2000 in every way. Even by then, China will still lag behind the major sports powers in the world of the 1970s and 1980s. However, conditions will be greatly improved to ensure the country's step-by-step rise to world-class level.

Experiences in world sports development have shown that while the development of sports is conditioned by the growth of national economy, the former may occur faster than the latter for a given country under certain conditions. China can make rapid progress by giving full play to the advantages of her socialist system, making a rational overall plan using her human, material, and financial resources in a concentrated manner, and training her athletes in a scientific way.

Experts both at home and abroad have predicted that by the end of the century, China will rank sixth in terms of economic strength, after the United States, the Soviet Union, Japan, the Federal Republic of Germany, and France, or possibly fifth, ahead of France. Such an economic basis makes it quite possible for China to attain her strategic goal of becoming a great sports power within the remaining 11 years of the century. By then, her sports skills and overall sports development may be up to the level of the other great sports powers. By mid-21st century, when her economy should be close to that of the leading developed countries and she is a thriving, modernized, powerful socialists state, China will not only be able to contend with the other great sports powers in sports skills, but should approach or equal them in overall sports development.

Strategic Measures to Promote Sport

The 21st century promises both a bright future and arduous tasks for China. Realizing the goal of becoming a world sports power calls for a series of strategic measures. Socialization and a scientific approach are the two wings that will enable China's sports to take off.

Chinese sports specialists have put forward the following comprehensive proposals:

- Vigorously carry out reforms of the sports system
- Deepen the understanding on the part of society of physical culture's importance; popularize sports knowledge and step up research into sports theory
- Vigorously improve popular physique so as to raise the quality of health of the population
- Attach strategic importance to winning gold medals at the Olympics and Asian Games
- Actively apply science to sports
- Improve the system of rewards to encourage young elite athletes to come forward
- Gradually increase investments in physical cultural work and apply more economic resources to make the sports financial structure pluralistic
- Make full use of stadiums and gymnasiums by making them accessible to the public
- Enact appropriate sports laws and regulations

At present, the reform of the physical cultural system is an urgent task. It is necessary to fully mobilize the various forces in society to make it possible to run physical culture in a more decentralized manner. Meanwhile, the government should adopt policies encouraging social organizations, collectives, and individuals to take part in the effort. It is necessary to build multilayered contingents of athletes in different forms and from various channels and to reform the system of training and competition so that in the future most of the top-notch teams will emerge from provincial capital cities, trades, enterprises, and colleges and universities. Efforts of different localities and trades and departments must be joined by breaking the boundaries between them and permitting sports talent to flow among them. The system of competition should be reformed so that all qualified sports teams have equal opportunities.

Coordinating the efforts of the nation as a whole and taking the Olympics and Asian Games as targets, preparations must be made for competitions in key events. Localities and units must make real efforts to train Olympic contenders in a concentrated and planned way. Physical culture education in schools and spare-time training, both of which are of strategic importance,

Future efforts will be made to improve athletic performance and increase the number of Chinese athletes stepping up to receive medals at international events.

should be strengthened. Conscientious efforts should be made to improve performance in track-and-field, swimming, and other events in which China is weak.

Science and technology are essential for improving sports. It is necessary to widely apply modern scientific theory and the latest technology to sports and to sports training in particular. It is necessary to strengthen sports schools and colleges, vigorously cultivate sports talent, and raise the general cultural and scientific level of sports professionals and the professional standards of coaches at different levels.

Summary

Looking forward to the 21st century, Chinese sports workers are resolved to blaze a new trail characteristic of China in sports development. Ancient arts such as wushu and modern sports such as diving will benefit from the application of new scientific discoveries. The future will also bring the fruits of the national government's concern to both increase and improve the effect that sport has on fitness, productivity, and culture itself. The future should bring China to a lofty position in the arenas of national and international sport.

Contributors

Editors

MA Qiwei (left), Howard G. KNUTTGEN (middle), and WU Zhongyuan (right).

Howard G. KNUTTGEN, PhD

Educated at Springfield College, Pennsylvania State University, and Ohio State University, Howard G. Knuttgen was a Fulbright Scholar at the University of Copenhagen. He is the director of the Center for Sports Medicine and professor of applied physiology at The Pennsylvania State University. Dr. Knuttgen is a past president of the American College of Sports Medicine and is currently cochairman of the Scientific Commission of the International Federation of Sports Medicine (FIMS). He has visited and toured China on seven occasions since 1980 to take part in scientific meetings, sports medicine activities, and cultural exchange. It was through his acquaintance with Dr. Ma that this book came to fruition.

MA Qiwei, PhD

A native of Fujian, Ma Qiwei graduated from Southwest Associated University, receiving his baccalaureate in psychology. He attended graduate school at Springfield College, Massachusetts, from which he received Master of Physical Education and Master of Education degrees. A professor at the Beijing Institute of Physical Education, Dr. Ma has served as chairperson of the China Society of Sport Psychology and vice director of the China Sports Science Society.

WU Zhongyuan, BL

A native of Shanghai, Wu Zhongyuan graduated from the Department of Law, Tong Ji University. He is presently director of the Press Commission of the Chinese Olympic Committee and is director of the China Olympic Publishing House. Mr. Wu also serves as vice-president of the China Sports Press Association and is an executive member of the International Press Association.

Authors

GU Shiquan

Mr. Gu graduated from the Shanghai Institute of Physical Education Graduate Department in 1959. He is presently an associate professor at the Beijing Institute of Physical Education, where he is also library director. He is presently secretary-general of the China Society of Sports History.

HUANG Zongcheng

Mr. Huang graduated from the graduate department of the Beijing Institute of Physical Education in 1959 with a specialization in human anatomy and biomechanics. He is the vice director of the National Research Institute of Sports Science in Beijing, a member of the executive board of the China Sports Science Society, and a director of the China Society of Biomechanics.

LIANG Zengshou

Having graduated from the Department of Information, Fudan University, in 1948, Mr. Liang is presently deputy director of the State Physical Education and Sports Commission. He has played an active role in the compilation of a book on Chinese sports in the year 2000 and has published several articles on the development of physical culture and sports in China. He is presently general secretary of the China Sports Development Study Society.

LIN Shuying

Graduating from the Department of Chinese Literature, Beijing Workers University, Ms. Lin was a member of the Chinese National Gymnastic Team in 1959 and, in 1960, was awarded the title Master of Sport. She has published a number of articles on sports research and presently serves as chief of the Research Office of the State Physical Education and Sports Commission.

LU Xianwu

Mr. Lu graduated from the foreign language department of Zhejiang Teachers College and presently serves as vice-director of the Policy Research Office of the State Physical Education and Sports Commission. He has translated and published a number of books on training, sport physiology, and sport lexicology.

QU Zonghu

A specialist in theory and teaching methods for school physical education, Mr. Qu's *Theories and Principles of Physical Education in School* has been published in six editions. He is an associate professor and vice-president at the Beijing Institute of Physical Education and serves as chairperson of the National Society of School Physical Education.

QUE Yongwu

Ms. Que has served as a women's coach of volleyball for over 25 years and as the coach of the national women's team for 15 years. She is the general secretary and a member of the executive board of the China Sports Science Society.

WANG Zeshan

Graduating in 1959 from the graduate department of the Shanghai Institute of Physical Education, Mr. Wang has published a number of articles on physical training theories and methods as well as physical education theory. He is presently a professor at the Beijing Institute of Physical Education and a board member of the China Sports Science Society.

WENG Qingzhang, MD

Dr. Weng is currently Professor of Sports Medicine at the National Research Institute of Sports Science, Beijing. He served as representative for sports medicine during the 1978 National Science Conference, at which time he was presented a Scientific Research Prize. He serves as deputy general secretary of the Chinese Association of Sports Medicine.

XIE Qionghuan

A graduate of the Shanghai Teachers University, Mr. Xie served as lecturer on the faculty of the Wuhan Institute of Physical Education. He participated in the compilation of a book on Chinese sports in the year 2000 and has published extensively on art and sports. He has served as editor-in-chief of the *Learned Journal*

and as director of the Sports Sociology Research Institute. At present, he is head of the Office of Sports Theory and serves as deputy general secretary of both the China Sports Development Studies Society and the China Sport Science Theory Society.

YANG Tianle, MD

Dr. Yang is a professor of exercise physiology and vice-director of the National Research Institute of Sports Science, Beijing. He serves as executive vice-president and general secretary of the Chinese Association of Sports Medicine. In 1987, he was a winner of a National Advanced Science and Technology prize.

YANG Zeyi, MD

An associate professor of sports medicine at the Institute of Sports Medicine, Beijing Medical University, Dr. Yang also serves as vice-director of the Doping Control Center at the National Research Institute of Sports Medicine, Beijing. He was a winner of the National Advanced Science and Technology prize.

Index

DATE DUE

APR 8 0 2001			
DEC 0 5 2001			

GAYLORD

PRINTED IN U.S.A.